Musings on Minutiae

Humorous Essays, Anecdotes, & Childhood Memories

Weston Locher

Published by Lulu.com
Edited by Anne Locher
Cover art and layout by Amanda Kent
Author photograph by Stephanie Rizzo

ISBN 978-0-557-22263-6

First Edition

www.musingsonminutiae.com

For my parents…
without whom, this book would
never have been written.

Mostly because of that whole birth thing.

Contents

Chapter 1:
   It's Funny 'Cause It's True

Chapter 2:
   Childhood Memories

Chapter 3:

> *Workin' for the Man or Woman —*
> *The Politically Correct Way to Title*
> *a Chapter About the Corporate World*

Chapter 4:

> *Cat Tales*

Chapter 5:

Sometimes My Imagination
Gets the Best of Me

Chapter 6:

Apartment Living, or 500 Square Feet
of White Walls and Sterility

Preface

For some reason, I feel the need to preface everything I do. I'm not sure if it's some sort of defense mechanism or if I'm just a huge control freak. Actually, now that I think about it, it's definitely because I'm a control freak. Before you dive into the following pages of hilarity, I wanted to set up exactly what you are about to get yourself into.

This is my book: a collection of observations, rants, anecdotes, and unbelievable childhood memories that for some reason I felt the need to share with the world, regardless of how often numerous acquaintances begged me not to. Maybe it's because I enjoy pushing my lunacy on others or maybe it's because whenever something truly bizarre would happen in my life, my mother would always say, "Remember that for your book!"

Well, Mom, I hope I remembered most of the good stuff.

Keep in mind that the following stories are meant to be purely humorous and any resemblances to actual persons are completely intended because it's infinitely funnier that way.

Midway through writing this, I realized three things: the first was that this page ended up as more of a disclaimer than an actual preface to the book. It didn't really set things up how I'd hoped and in reality, it was just a random page that pointed out several of my insecurities and included a shout out to my mother whom, rather than simply acknowledge in print, I should probably pick up a phone and call once in a while. Subsequently, this made me realize that I should write an actual preface for the book. Thirdly, with that in mind I realized that in a strange twist of fate I just prefaced the preface of my own book.

Real Preface

My father always used to say that my generation would grow up with a bad case of attention deficit disorder. Now, admittedly he's said a lot of really crazy, insane, and downright unintelligible things over the years, but this was one statement on which he stood firm. He started on this tirade years before they switched ADD into the more popular version, ADHD, or Attention Deficit Hyperactivity Disorder which caused millions of children around the nation to be carted to the doctor's office and given yet another placebo prescription.

Dad would explain that because we were raised in a world full of technology, something that was nonexistent when he was growing up, this would cause our overall attention spans to be decreased to mere seconds and we would not be able to focus on any one thing for very long and thus not become a functional member of society. Keep in mind that all of this infinite wisdom came from the same man who claimed that growing up he had to walk to school in the snow uphill both ways without shoes or a jacket, all while carrying his thirty-six textbooks and dragging rabid anarchist Eskimos behind him who, interestingly enough, also didn't dress for the weather. You know the story. I'm sure your fathers said it too, though it's likely that their versions were a bit more plausible.

I don't believe that my father was completely correct in his thinking. I'm pretty sure that I grew up relatively normal and have come to be quite proud of my ability to focus and multi-task. Of course, it's possible that I'm blinded from the truth and I can see how his suspicions may explain the format of this book.

This is not a novel. This is not a coherent story that contains a deep plot, detailed character development, a tragic love triangle, or a surprising twist at the end. This is not a novelization of the 1997 summer blockbuster movie, *Titanic*, though don't be surprised if somewhere along the line, a colossal boat sinks and thousands of people die. This is not a work of fiction. Now that I think about it, this isn't really non-fiction either. I'm riding a really fine line with this book. I never read non-fiction growing up because books about elves and robots appealed to me more than reading about history and dead people who changed the world. This book does, however, make references to robots on several occasions. Mostly this is just a collection of completely random stories, insights, and anecdotes that I have seen or experienced throughout my life thus far, and then one night, during an inebriated episode of arguing with my judgmental cat, decided to share with the world. The tales contained herein are reasonably short and scattered and sometimes drift off into strange places. Do I believe that this is an indication that I somehow developed symptoms of the fabled ADD, ADHD, or ABCDEFG along the way? Of course not! It just means that I…. Wait, what was I talking about?

Chapter 1:
It's Funny 'Cause It's True

Birthdays:
Then and Now

Did you ever realize how when you're younger, birthdays are all about making memories with your friends, but once you get older they become about your friends coercing you into drinking so much that you don't remember anything?

I attended a close friend's birthday party over the weekend and it really got me thinking about how different the parties were growing up. The way I recall it is that first, you would pray that your birthday fell on a weekend so that you didn't have to go to school on the day of. Next, you would try to convince your parents to let three to four of your rambunctious buddies come over to your place for a sleep over. After you spent a good amount of time whining, crying, and threatening to hold your breath until you passed out, they would eventually buckle and at that point they had succumbed to two very hard-to-swallow facts. One: they were not going to get any sleep that night, and two: you were going to raise hell.

The evening would begin with the ceremonial ordering of the pizza, which you and your friends would gobble up in a matter of minutes, and then proceed to guzzle down thirty-six gallons of Mountain Dew. (It was only later in life that I would realize that caffeine gives me a sour stomach, and that I am lactose intolerant; thus all of that cheese pizza had been slowly tearing me apart from the inside. You live and you learn, I guess.) Shortly after the clock struck ten and the sugar rush kicked in, there was only one thing to do: all-night video game marathon! What followed for the parents were eight sleepless hours listening to juvenile name-calling and prepubescent screaming. Those nights were the best.

Now that I'm older, the paradigm has shifted, and birthdays are approached a bit differently. First, you pray that the day after your birthday falls on a weekend so that you don't have to go to work hung over. Next, you try to convince your girlfriend to go out to a bar to celebrate with seven or eight of your rambunctious buddies. After you spend a good amount of time whining, crying, and threatening to hold your breath until you pass out (wow, some things never change), she eventually buckles. At that point you have succumbed to two very eye-opening facts. One: you are going to spend more money than you have available in your bank account, and two: your friends are going to embarrass the crap out of you. The evening begins with the traditional ordering of various types of liquor shots, with the most ridiculous of names, followed by a toast to your good health, and swift consumption of said alcohol. Shortly after the clock strikes three in the morning and all of your deepest secrets from the last year have been revealed publicly, there's only one thing to do: round up your closest friends into some vehicles and head back to your place for the after party! What follows is you passing out on the couch while your friends take turns drawing obscene pictures on your face with a Sharpie marker. These nights are the best. At least, I think they are. I can't remember.

Heat Stroke: 763,
My Father: 0

For as long as I can remember, my father has had a knack for getting heat stroke almost anywhere he goes: on family vacations, while running errands, during his workday, and while sitting very still in air-conditioned rooms.

My dad suffers from a disease called "Man Pride Syndrome" and often gets himself into situations that call for someone to stand up, take charge, and be the alpha male. The results of these actions typically end up causing him to stand outside in direct sunlight for long periods of time. Years ago when my sister had enrolled in graduate school we had to move her from our home in Ohio into an apartment in Kansas City, Missouri. We took two vehicles and started out on the long haul in the middle of August. Just one exit away from Kansas City, my sister's car developed a sense of humor and thought it would be hilarious to break down on the interstate. She coasted it off the road and onto an exit ramp where we quickly realized that we needed to call a tow truck and have it taken to a local shop. Within a short walking distance was a gas station and, as the temperature had surpassed the hundred-degree mark, we decided to wait in the air-conditioned store for help to arrive. Suddenly my father's Man Pride Syndrome flared up something fierce and he told us to stay inside and he would go stand with the car and wait so as to protect it from being the target of nefarious deeds that he concocted in his mind. We tried to convince him that this was not necessary as we were on a fairly desolate road and in fact, my sister's broken-down heap was the only vehicle we could see for miles. This would not do so he left the store to stand with the car out in the blazing sun.

Over the course of the next hour, my mother, sister and I all stood at the window watching him. As locals came and went from the store, they would pause to see what we were so focused on. It appeared that my father had become something of a local attraction as men and women would return to the gas stations with their husbands and wives to watch him as well. Slowly but surely as his body began to soak up ultraviolet rays, he began to slump over the side of the car, sinking lower and lower as he sought shade in the back bumper region. Thankfully the towing folks arrived before he had completely melted into a puddle of tourist clothing and comb-over hair.

He took the remainder of the day to recover and eventually we made it to Kansas City. With his Man Pride Syndrome still raging, we proceeded to haul all of my sister's belongings up the stairs to her third-floor apartment. The weather was still as hot as ever, and by the end of the day my dad had to concede victory to the heat stroke a second time. It was only much later that he learned the best way to get his body back to a normal temperature was to dunk his head into a cooler full of ice. This made for some great pictures in the family albums.

These are only two examples of times that he tried to spontaneously combust, and because of its frequency we can no longer as a family say, "Do you remember the time that Dad got really bad heat stroke?" and all be revisiting the same memory in our minds.

101 Ways to Hurt Yourself: A Children's Guide to Recess

Schoolyard playgrounds used to be dangerous places. The key words there are "used," "to," and "be." I'm a believer that the higher the danger levels on a playground, the higher the coolness factor. School boards around the country don't seem to share my point of view.

Over the Christmas holidays I visited my parents in Ohio where I grew up. During one of my trips out into the frozen tundra, I stopped by my old elementary school. I hadn't been on the premises in over fourteen years and truth be told, had no desire to go; however, I had my girlfriend with me and she has mastered the art of getting me to do things that I really don't want to do. While she thought it would be cute to see where I spent my mischievous youth, I tried telling her that it was just like any other school and I was doubtful that anything had changed. As I got out of the car and braved the snow, I noticed something truly horrific. All of the old playground equipment that I had spent six years of my life climbing up, falling off, climbing up a second time, falling off again, and subsequently hurting myself on, had been torn down and replaced by brightly colored, child-proof plastic eyesores.

I had not prepared myself for a change of this magnitude. I stood in shock while I gazed out over an alien land of snow-covered plastic. At some point in the last fourteen years, everything that I once knew had disappeared. I felt as though I had lost a part of my childhood. After all, this was the place where I'd had my first meaningful conversation with a female, it was the site of a football's first encounter with my groin, and above all, it was the location where I was first punched in the face by a bully. Somewhere out there, a tooth of mine lay deep within the soil.

Looking back, I remember recess as a time of freedom and unpredictability, though more often than not, it was also a time of unbridled violence. You never knew exactly what was going to happen but undoubtedly, someone would do something stupid and get hurt. As kids we spent our time trying to burn off our excess energy by running, climbing, and falling, all while trying to avoid the playground attendant who, if I remember correctly, looked eerily similar to the Bride of Frankenstein. During my time as a student there, I saw many of my peers succumb to the evils of the equipment. It was commonplace for someone to bust their head open on a merry-go-round or nose-dive off the side of a slide and end up unconscious. I suppose it's kind of like being in a war and you just get used to the carnage after a while. As the old memories flooded over me, I couldn't help but feel bad for anyone who was currently a student there. With a playground like the fluorescent one I saw, I had no doubts that their recess time was boring and uneventful. The experiences I'd had on that playground helped shape me into who I am today… and caused most of the scars found on my body.

I felt sorry for the current student body as by no fault of their own, they were doomed to grow up in a time where children are coddled and live inside a constant bubble of safety. I felt remorseful that they would never know what it was like to take a ride on a tire swing hanging from rusted chains that would snap if you piled on too many buddies and gained too much velocity. I was saddened that they were never going to experience the joy of an aluminum slide that would heat up in the summer, causing your skin to fuse itself to the metal, and leaving a trail of blood and sizzling meat behind as you slid down. I was regretful that they would never swing from the monkey bars that stood ten feet off the ground, giving concussions to all those who attempted to cross and failed. I was disappointed at the fact that they would never find themselves on a rotted seesaw that without warning would break into two pieces, causing them and a friend to simultaneously break their tail bones in three places. I was mournful that they would never feel the freedom of jumping off a swing and having their shirt get stuck in the chain, ripping it clean off their bodies in mid flight. Above all, I was heavyhearted that they would never know the feeling of having a shirtless friend land on them after jumping off that same swing.

Condiment Commitment

In recent years I have acquired an affinity for barbecue sauce. It has become my favorite condiment and I prefer to have it handy during the majority of my meals whether it be fries, burgers, onion rings, you name it. I find that everything is twice as delicious with barbecue representing as my main dipping sauce. I love it so much that I've often fantasized about slathering some onto the back of my hand and taking a bite. But I wouldn't actually do that. That would be crazy.

There was a day in recent memory when I discovered that the rest of the world does not share my views on the sauce. During a recent trip to one of the major fast food vendors, who shall remain nameless but can easily be figured out as I drop subtle hints throughout this column, I ordered a burger and some fries. While waiting in my car to get to the pick-up window, I sat and thought about how wonderful this was all going to taste once I had added the barbecue sauce to the mix. When I finally got to the window, the lady handed me my drink and the bag of food and asked me if I would like any ketchup with my order. I politely declined her request and asked if I could instead have some barbecue sauce to go along with my meal. This caused her to awkwardly freeze up. She looked as though I had just stuck a gun in her face and demanded money from the company safe. Several seconds later she broke eye contact, turned away and softly spoke the following statement: "I'm sorry sir, barbecue sauce does not come with that meal." For the record, that quote has since been added to my ongoing "Most Ridiculous Things Anyone Has Ever Said to Me" list.

My response to her was a simple "Why the hell not?" which was followed by a heated tirade about how barbecue sauce should come with every meal served anywhere in the entire world. She continued to stand in the window, wide-eyed and frozen stiff at my reaction. I realized that in my excitement I had gotten a little bit loud and before I knew it, another restaurant employee came to the window and politely asked me what the problem was. He claimed that he was the manager of the restaurant, and since they consider themselves to be "way better than fast food," it was his prerogative to make sure that my visit was the best that it could be. I apologized for getting loud with the gal and shared with him that all I really wanted was some barbecue sauce with my order. He nodded, said he understood, and then asked me to wait a moment while he checked my order. The drive-thru window slid shut as he wandered off. I assumed that he was going to either grab the sauce or call the police to come pick up the crazy person who was temporarily shutting down his drive-thru.

A minute later, the window slid back open. The manager told me that he had "investigated my order" and regretted to inform me that barbecue sauce was not available with that particular combination of food. He suggested that if I were to go ahead and order the chicken nuggets, then I would be more than welcome to have up to two sides of barbecue sauce.

I did not respond and instead sat silently, staring him right in the eyes, my left eyelid twitching intermittently. At least, on the outside it probably looked as if I was simply staring at him when in reality I was holding my breath and trying to make his head explode with my mind. He seemed to realize that chicken nuggets were not going to be the solution to the problem and took drastic measures to ensure my happiness as a customer. He thought a moment, and then he smiled, called me "Buddy" and offered me what he referred to as "an awesome deal." He said that it was my lucky day and he would give me containers of barbecue sauce for just ten cents apiece.

While driving away from the window in my frustrated state, I couldn't help but let out a deep laugh as though I had just heard the world's funniest joke. In the end I hadn't succeeded in getting my barbecue sauce. I had, however, succeeded in accidentally driving off without paying for my meal.

For Argument's Sake

I enjoy a good argument. More than the actual act itself, I like to *win* the argument. Especially when I know that I'm right. I enjoy worthy opponents who put up a good debate. The topic can be anything, and if I am not well versed in the subject, it's easy for me to get caught up in the moment and I will make up reasons to argue for or against it on the fly. Some people are quick to point out that I antagonize those around me in hopes of sparking an altercation. I agree with that statement.

If I chose to, I could blame my love of bickering on my upbringing. I sure got enough practice against an older and more seasoned sister. We would go back and forth about anything under the sun. These bouts usually took place in the back seat of my mother's minivan where she and my father acted as both audience members and judges for the competition. If my mother turned around and said, "Hey! Leave your brother alone!" then I had won the battle. If she exclaimed, "Stop provoking her!" then my sister sat in the winner's circle. If my father turned around, lips foaming with spittle and yelled, "Don't make me turn this car around!" then we considered it a draw. We stopped having draws when one day my father turned around in the driver's seat and lashed back at us in some kind of mid-ride spanking attempt. As expected, we soon crashed into the car in front of us. In my youth when I failed to win a case, I could always throw myself on the floor and claim that she had violently knocked me down, and my parents would generally believe me. This tactic worked up until she moved away for college. Since the days of lying on the floor sobbing are now behind me, I have to rely on a quick mind and sharp tongue to get the job done. Mostly I blame my high school for this passion of mine. Unlike most normal academies we didn't have a debate team, which I would have joined and probably thrived in, and therefore didn't get the quarrel bug out of my system earlier in life like I was able to with such wedgie-inducing extracurricular activities as theater and orchestra.

As a general rule of thumb, if someone likes to argue then those around suggest that he or she eventually become a lawyer. I don't agree with this reasoning at all. There's a difference between making a convincing argument and bickering for the sake of winning. I'm of the mindset that if you love to argue, then you might be better suited as a used car salesman. I feel confident that I could argue with and verbally pummel almost anyone into driving that new Ford home off the lot.

Recently my squabbling hit an all-time low. There are occasions at work when I do not agree with a certain policy or procedure and don't hesitate to make it known. If I'm aware of the correct solution to a problem, I will be vocal towards anyone who tries to say differently. In a recent meeting I disagreed with a co-worker's plan of action towards handling a new process. Having years of experience in the department, I stuck to my guns on what I had learned and knew to be a better way. Not even wanting to hear his suggestion in full, I was overcome with the familiar adrenaline rush of a man ready to verbally brawl. We went back and forth for a bit, both convinced that we were in the right. I had made my bullet points to support my theories and listed them out several times to alleviate all doubt to those around us. My adversary then explained his master plan to the room, using descriptive detail and counterpoints. While he and I regrouped, everyone sat in silence for a few moments. Round one was officially complete. Suddenly and without warning the rest of the managers announced that they agreed with my ideas and that's the way we would proceed. I found myself scoffing at the debate's being over so quickly. Like always, I was right, but I was not satisfied in the least. I had cleared my schedule so that this argument could last for at least another forty-five minutes. I was counting on this to be an epic knock-down-drag-out for the ages... but it wasn't.

In just under five minutes, the jury had announced the verdict and they tried to continue on with other matters but I wasn't having it. In that moment I made a strategic decision that would keep the tiff going and I did the unthinkable: I shifted sides and began arguing against my own initial argument, taking my former opponent's side and making him an ally. As I began to plead a new case, I was met with open mouths and looks of disbelief. Even my associate was caught off guard by my actions and stared in horror as I began to ramble. My immediate manager held up his hand to stop me. "We're moving on," he said and brought about the next order of business. Full of discontent, I stood up and stormed out of the room in search of another opponent. It was time to bandy words with anyone at the water cooler who had an opinion I didn't agree with.

Fear and Loathing in the Roller Skating Rink

Several weeks ago I made the decision to go roller-skating. In retrospect, I realize now that at my age, this should have been very low on my list of things to do on a Friday night.

My girlfriend and I, along with a couple of our friends, decided that roller skating would be a good way to kill an evening and tempt fate, so off we went, eager to repeatedly circle a room with wheels strapped to our feet. Apparently everyone else on planet Earth also wanted to tempt fate and the place was packed tighter than free cheeseburger day at McDonald's. Upon entering the building I wished that I had brought a machete along in order to hack my way through an invisible wall of teenage hormones that was pouring out through the door. Once we were in and the skates were on, we headed towards the floor. The couple that we arrived with tried to out-cool us by bringing their own roller blades. We didn't know that they were one step away from being professional skaters and would spend the next hour making us look like the biggest amateurs in the room.

A bunch of kids was blocking the way onto the skating area, which meant that instead of bracing myself against a wall while I got my footing, I just had to go for it and hope for the best. Throughout the night it was difficult to think of anything besides how the roller skating experience had changed since I was a kid. After being inside for only ten minutes, I could tell that they did things a lot differently nowadays. Admittedly, some elements of the roller skating experience had remained the same. They still had a snack bar in which all of their foods contained hot dog in some form or fashion, they still had a slew of arcade games tucked away in the back for those kids with poor balance and inner ear problems, and the make-out corner was still located in the darkest section of the room, which growing up, I was never invited to.

The things that had changed were what really amazed me. People were skating in massive lines together, taking up the majority of the floor, which back in my day would have gotten you kicked out. These lines made it nearly impossible to pass anyone, especially when you didn't want to leave the security of the wall. It was a comfort to me knowing that there was something solid to grab onto should things start to go south. Another oddity I noticed was that many of the kids were skating around with what appeared to be some sort of pacifier in their mouths that flashed rainbow colors. The adult in me could only think about how much it would hurt should they fall on their face and have it jammed halfway down their trachea. When you're a child, ignorance really is bliss. Lastly, there seemed to be a new trend of taking digital cameras out onto the skating floor in order to snap quick pictures of their buddies for an in-progress Best Friends Forever collage. It wasn't bad enough that I was trying to stay on my feet and avoid running into anyone, but now I had to deal with constant camera flashes temporarily blinding me every two to three minutes. Somewhere out there, I'm sure that there's a photo of three teenage girls skating together, smiling and holding hands and somewhere in the background there I am with a surprised look on my face, accidentally body checking a six year old.

It's quite possible that some of the skaters were unhappy that my crew of ragtag, legal-age skaters was upsetting the demographic of the room. There was a young fellow perched along the wall, watching everyone enjoy the skating experience and each time I shuffled my way by him, he made it a point to scream loudly at me as if he were trying to intimidate a bear into leaving a camp site. I thought maybe it was just one of those crazy fads that kids are into these days but then I noticed that he never did it to anyone else. Another guy who was infinitely more adept at skating than I had apparently made it his mission to knock me over. He made two failed attempts but on his third trip around, he slammed into me, causing me to flail into my girlfriend, which ended up with us both on the floor. I immediately had flashbacks to my youth where my mother would make me wear an elastic band to keep my glasses on my face. It looked ridiculous, but she knew how clumsy I was.

Once I recovered from the fall, I filled with rage and started formulating my revenge plan. Before I could take any action, I found myself stuck behind an impassable line of teenage girls that reminded me vaguely of the Berlin Wall. As I was uncomfortably pinned between a group of sixth graders to my rear and a teenage girl whose shirt read "Boy Hater" to the front, I decided to call off the revenge, get off the floor, and call it a night.

The Emergency Vehicles Will Arrive... Eventually

A few days ago, a fellow employee from the office and I were out running a business-related errand. We were discussing life, politics, and how much we both despise the local traffic. It seems that there was a law put into effect at some point that requires everyone to take crazy pills before they are allowed to get behind the wheel of a car. Some people take the bare minimum while other people clearly overdose.

I see people in this town do a lot of crazy things while I am out and about, but some drivers just throw caution to the wind and look out for themselves regardless of the situation at hand. Being in a major metropolitan area, we have a lot of traffic. This mathematical formula is so simple here that even I can reason it out without a calculator. Lots of traffic plus lots of stupid people on the roads plus a lot of stupid choices plus a ton of accidents equals lots of clowns crying... I mean, equals the constant need for emergency vehicles to be absolutely everywhere.

From my understanding, emergency vehicles are out to help people. Whether it be the police, an ambulance, or a fire truck, when their lights are on and the sirens are blaring, they are headed somewhere to help someone who is either dying, on fire, or being eaten by gerbils. This is common sense. When you hear the sirens coming, the proper protocol is to locate the direction they are coming from, and get the heck out of the way. What blows my mind is that around here, people do not attempt to locate where the sirens are coming from, nor do they attempt to get out of the way. So much so, that you regularly see emergency vehicles hopping the median and rocketing down the opposite side of the road as their only hope of getting where they are headed. Maybe it's that people don't care, or maybe they have their awful reggaeton music blasting so loud that they don't hear the sirens in the first place.

My co-worker and I were sitting at an intersection waiting for the green turn arrow when all of a sudden, cue the sirens. As always, I rolled down my window and attempted to find out which direction they were coming from. To my right there was a giant semi truck blocking my view. Since I couldn't spot the emergency vehicle, I assumed it was coming from that general direction. At the same time, the lanes across the intersection from me got their green light and a flood of cars and trucks made a break for it. It was right around this time that I lost my mind and began to foam at the mouth. Somewhere, someone was probably being attacked by a flock of rabid pigeons and all these other drivers were just going about their day, completely unconcerned with letting the police or ambulance through the intersection. My co-worker joined me in my rant as we agreed that the other drivers were useless to society and should they ever be in need of a fire truck when their home is ablaze, they won't be happy when some jerk in a car wasn't moving to let it come to the rescue. I could hear the sirens getting closer and was still in awe that no one had made way for them. It was right around this time that I happened to glance in my rear-view mirror and noticed the line of police vehicles, lights flashing, behind me. Like a ton of bricks, it hit me. I was the one blocking all of the police cars.

There was one car between the police and me. It was a red SUV that began to pull up on the median to let them through. Since traffic was still flowing through the intersection and the giant semi continued to block me to my right, I followed suit and also pulled up on the median in hopes that they could squeeze by me. I checked my rear view mirror a second time right as the red SUV popped on its undercover police lights. Not only had I been blocking a line of police cars, but also I had successfully blocked them a second time as they tried to get around me. I had become that guy. I was now the person that all the other drivers were talking bad about. I had done the one thing that I hate the most. Suddenly, a girl in a fancy ball gown, decked out in lots of diamonds ran up to my open car window and handed me my Hypocrite of the Year award.

And Now a Word from Our Sponsors

I find television advertisements to be an excellent source of humor. While most folks in this day and age are busy fast-forwarding through commercial breaks with their magic Digital Video Recorder boxes, I occasionally stop to watch, mostly to find out what products are currently being pushed upon unsuspecting consumers.

Fifty percent of the ads you see during commercials are for new fuel-efficient cars that look cool, go fast, and have a built-in iPod connector that comes standard. Another forty-five percent of the ad block belongs to cell phones or cell phone related services. We're shown which company has the latest and greatest in touch-screen technology and how it can run helpful applications, access the Internet, tie your shoes, and occasionally even make a phone call.

Now, the other five percent of commercial time is where things start to get a little crazy. Usually, this other percentage belongs to the local advertisements. You know, the ones where the volume on your TV kicks itself up ten notches and blows your dad's hairpiece against the wall behind the couch. These are the low-budget ads that look like a colorblind prison inmate in solitary confinement edited them. You'll spot ads for legal counsels, such as our local personal injury attorneys, Sheckler, Sheckler, Sheckler, and Brooks. It's one of those ads where The Shecklers get thirty seconds to beg for your legal business all while making Brooks feel bad that he has a different father. Or maybe you're familiar with your local car dealer's ad, where the creepy old used car salesman shoves his youngest daughter in front of the camera in an attempt to sell a few beat up Saabs and attract the attention of perverts in a ten-mile radius.

There are other times when this five percent is filled with a national advertisement that just feels downright out of place. For example, a few nights ago I was enjoying a special on the Discovery Channel about a group of people who were making a documentary about hating television. Sure, it was a little hypocritical, but that's not the point of this story. Several minutes in the commercial break kicks into full effect and I am treated to a crazy advertisement about a new vehicle called The Cube. It's essentially a tiny little box with wheels that induces claustrophobia in the driver. It also comes in blue. The fifteen-second commercial was full of swirling colors and pounding dance music. Though it was marketed to get me interested in possibly purchasing the car, it really just made me want to have a seizure. The next advertisement was for a company offering cellular phone ring tones. In quick succession, a slew of horrible song snippets by horrible artists that my phone could blare out whenever it rang came at me like a sonic assault. I opted not to join the service and lost a little more faith in popular music.

Then it was time for the weird advertisement. After having all of my senses beaten into submission and spit on by the previous commercials, I was quite surprised that the final ad was for Duke's Mayonnaise. Yes, you read that correctly. Mayonnaise. Backed by a soundtrack that would have won a Grammy in the 1940s, slow-moving elderly folks spreading mayo onto denture-friendly sandwiches replaced my world of colors, sounds, shapes, and general sensory overload. I know the mobile phone world is booming and the automotive industry is in the toilet, but what warrants getting Duke's Mayonnaise, the secret of great Southern cooks, onto my television screen? Apparently I didn't fit into the ad's target demographic. My curiosity diminished, however, as David Maus's used car advertisement came on, raising my television volume to eighty, and subsequently hurtling me across the room into a wall, knocking me unconscious.

My Corrugated Plastic Hell

Driving home from work one day I found myself behind an old pickup truck, which every five hundred feet or so, would stop and the driver would turn on the emergency blinkers, climb out of the driver's seat with a plastic sign in hand, leisurely make his way to the opposite side of the car and then plant the sign into the ground near the sidewalk. After completing his mission he would make the long journey back to the driver's side, climb into the cab and continue on his way. Since this was all taking place during the heart of rush hour, a time when local motorists who are full of road rage are leaving work with the goal of getting home or ending your life and theirs in a fiery blaze of twisted metal, there was no way I was going to be able to casually cruise around him and continue on my way.

After his third stop, I started paying attention to the sign he was dropping. It was one of those white corrugated plastic signs that people post at busy intersections to advertise goods or services such as homes for rent, garage sales, and budget crime scene cleanups. The sign dropped by the driver read "El Cheap-O Computer Repair... we'll fix your computer for Cheap.... O!" It was all very clever. Clearly there was a lot of time and effort put into creating such a spectacular catch phrase. I also noticed that there was a phone number at the bottom of the sign. On the driver's fourth stop, I was starting to join in on the local road rage mindset. In a moment of blind frustration, I pulled out my cell phone and dialed the number listed on the sign. While he was sauntering back to the driver's seat, I saw the man pull out a phone and answer it. A voice in my ear greeted me with "El Cheap-O computer repair, this is Jose." To which I responded, "Hi Jose…. DRIVE!"

.

The Toothpaste Aisle

I'm the type of person who, when I find something that I like, I generally stick with it. At restaurants, I'm the guy who always orders the same thing at each establishment. At bars, I'm the guy who always orders the same drink to start the night. At the vending machine, I'm the guy who immediately goes for the Dr. Pepper before checking out all the available options. At social gatherings, I'm the guy who always avoids the couple who brought their baby along; however, this is mainly for everyone's safety and well-being.

It's not that I'm neurotic; it's just that I know what I like, and I like reliability.

The previous statement may lead you to believe that my life is routine and boring, but you would be wrong and naive to think so. In my life of knowing what I like, there's always one thing that can be counted on to spice things up and add a dash of variety, spontaneity, and uncertainty just when I need it. It's called the toothpaste aisle. It can be found in nearly every supermarket across the world... except maybe in Britain. Now, I may be crazy, but I always feel like my regular grocery store has a constant rotation of new and exciting toothpaste brands and flavors. Because of this revolving door, I have never gotten accustomed to one particular kind of toothpaste; thus I face challenging decisions on each visit. It seems that new kinds of mouth soap are constantly being brought to market and to be honest, I'm having trouble keeping up. We have our pastes that whiten, and some that freshen breath; others are all about enamel strengthening, and some boast about being fluoride treated. I'm pretty sure there's even a brand that will stay home and tend to your pets while you're on vacation. Needless to say, there are numerous options.

What's important to me in a toothpaste is the taste. Or better yet, the lack of taste. What it comes down to is, I want something that isn't going to make the process of brushing my teeth any more of a time consuming burden than I already feel it to be. I don't want something that tastes so sweet and sugary that I might mistake it for candy while I'm sleepwalking late one night, and I'm done messing around with any toothpastes that look even remotely like they might have a cinnamon flavor. The last time I purchased red toothpaste on a whim, my eyes welled up, my face flushed, and I had a moment where I was absolutely positive that I was brushing my teeth with minced jalapeño peppers. This caused me to waste even more precious time cleaning my bathroom mirror as I had expectorated the burning mouthful upon contact. I prefer something that's neutral. Apparently I'm on the hunt for the Switzerland of toothpastes. In fact, I'm going to write a letter to someone and suggest that the companies begin printing a Swiss flag on these boxes just to make life easier for me.

Better yet, give me a "try before you buy" option with toothpastes. Normally during my trips to the grocery store, I see little old ladies strategically placed on the ends of aisles, championing samples of whatever new dinner will be fast and convenient for soccer moms to make. These grandmothers lure you in with their sweet, old-fashioned charm and promises of hard candy, and next thing you know, there you are sampling green bean casserole before realizing mid-chew that you hate green beans! Instead, let's set sweet ol' Edna up with a toothpaste station so she can help me find out which flavor works best for me and my lifestyle. I'm sure she'd plead a convincing argument for whatever brand she uses to clean her dentures. Let me brush, swish, and spit right there in the store with several different brands so that I may go home, secure in my toothpaste purchase. Though, when I get home, I'll notice that Edna also convinced me to purchase the economy size tub of green bean casserole. She's a crafty lass.

Fasten Your Seat Belt
and Hold On Tight, Grandma

About once a year my parents come to visit me in Florida so that we can spend some quality time together. Mostly I think it's so they can mess up my daily routine for several days. On their most recent trip, not only did they bring their suitcases, cameras, and obligatory tourist clothing, but they also brought my 80-year-old grandmother.

One of the days they were in town, my parents suggested that we visit Disney's Animal Kingdom since I live close by. They had visited the park a year prior and were anxious to go back for another visit. For those who don't keep up on Disney current events, which I'm assuming is pretty much anyone reading this, the Animal Kingdom is a park dedicated to showing off exotic animals that you don't normally see in Florida, or the United States in general. Spread out between the animal displays and food pavilions are a bunch of crazy rides and attractions.

With my family members and girlfriend in tow, we headed over to the park, visited as many areas as we could, and by the end of the day there was only one sector left to visit on our way out: Dino-Land. Within this prehistoric section of the park, we found a ride cleverly titled "Dinosaur!" that my father insisted was something we could do together as a family even though my fragile grandma looked doubtful. My mother assured her that she had been on the ride during her previous visit to the park and couldn't remember it at all; therefore, it couldn't be too crazy.

The warning sign at the beginning of the line queue mentioned that visitors shouldn't ride if they were afraid of the dark, experienced motion sickness, had heart problems, or were less than four feet tall. This put us in a bit of a predicament because my grandmother is not only afraid of the dark, but she experiences horrible motion sickness, has a pacemaker, and is absurdly short. For some reason we came together as a family and assured her that she would be just fine to go on the ride with us and didn't have anything to worry about. Once in the holding area we were shown a video to give some sort of back-story and purpose to the four-minute adventure we were about to embark on. I didn't catch the whole story, as I was preoccupied listening to my grandma muttering to herself in the dark saying, "I don't know if this is a good idea…"

We boarded the car and were instructed to buckle our seat belts and hold on tight. Call me a cynic, but those usually aren't the type of instructions that one is given before a nice, relaxing ride. Our futuristic vehicle then sped off down a tunnel and into a hallway containing lots of flashing lights. It was right around this point that the vehicle started shaking violently, something it would continue to do for the duration of the ride. We whirled, swooped, and gyrated our way through tunnels and were faced with robotic dinosaurs jumping out of the dark and into our faces every few seconds, causing my entire family to shriek at the top of their lungs each and every time. Everyone in the car was terrified and being thrown about violently. I found it hard to enjoy the ride, as I was preoccupied with worry for my grandmother's life, something I felt one of us had an obligation to do. I had gone into this with all family members alive and was rather determined not to leave with four adults and a corpse. I wasn't sure that Disney even had a protocol for that type of situation. As we were being shaken like dice in a Yahtzee cup, I could only imagine that the ride translated a feeling similar to the ones that the dinosaurs experienced as the asteroid was vaporizing them into extinction.

In the end, we survived the ride. Even Grandma. I could tell that she hadn't been prepared for what we experienced and was harboring nasty thoughts towards the rest of us for sweet talking her into climbing aboard. We left the park in the same manner that we leave nearly every family event… in uncomfortable silence.

Chapter 2:
Childhood Memories

Philadelphia, and Other Cities Dominated by Parking Meters

F amily vacations are never normal for anyone growing up, and the one my family took to Philadelphia, Pennsylvania, was no exception. I remember this vacation in particular because it was the first time I saw the Liberty Bell, the first time I saw Independence Hall, and the first time I almost died.

Parking for the historic district sites in Philly were unbelievably bad and more often than not the only spots you could get were controlled by the dreaded parking meters. What sticks out in my memory more than seeing the various sights around the city is my father having to drop everything and rush across town to refill the parking meter every thirty minutes. We would be watching speeches from actors dressed up as famous figures and in the middle of their orations my dad would glance at his watch, his face would go a sickly pale, and he would dash out the nearest door or window to go feed the meter.

With the heat being at an all-time high that summer and my father nearly keeling over from heat stroke, an act that he would attempt to re-create on every vacation thereafter, we decided to stop in a local park to cool off and plan our next course of action. The park was home to some beautiful flowers, some not-so-beautiful homeless guys, and a gigantic fountain. Since I had been complaining of the heat myself, my mother suggested that maybe I try to get close to the fountain and splash some of the cool water onto myself. The ground at the base of the fountain was rather wet and quite muddy, but conveniently placed around it were several small green rubber mats. She advised that I step on one of the mats so as not to dirty my shoes. I took her advice and leapt for one of them. As luck would have it, I hopped onto the mat that was apparently covering a hole leading directly to the center of the earth.

Before I knew it, I was waist deep and sinking fast. My mother was shrieking, my sister was shrieking, the homeless guys were laughing, and my father was nowhere to be found, likely out searching for change to fill the parking meter. Eventually they were able to wrestle me out of what nearly became another historic landmark.

Angry Felines, and Other Animals You Don't Want Hanging Off Your Face

O nce during a party thrown by my parents I learned two very important lessons. One: do not force a cat into a box against its will, and two: people will not show sympathy if you are injured due to your own stupidity. It's a shame that these lessons were learned only after the cat was already clinging to my face.

I can't say that I remember the event that brought friends and family members to our home that day, but I do remember that we were all in the garage talking when a young me, desperate for attention, decided that I would stuff my cat into an empty refrigerator box and stand it up on end, trapping her in a prison of cardboard. I believed that this would be an amusing stunt, not thinking of the emotional damage the cat was likely to suffer. She began to scratch, whine, and jump in her feeble attempts to escape. Eventually someone at the party, who had obviously left their sense of humor at home, mentioned how cruel and mean my actions were, so I tilted the box over to peek inside and make sure my cat was holding up all right.

As the large box tipped down far enough where I could see inside, I was greeted by a pair of feral glowing yellow eyes rushing up the box towards me like an out-of-control semi truck. In a moment of panic, I let go of the box, causing it to fall to the ground, but by then it was too late. The cat had already leapt for her freedom. Suddenly I felt a sharp pain in my mouth region and realized the horrible truth: the cat was officially dangling from my lower lip with one claw.

I did what anyone would do in my situation and started screaming bloody murder and shaking my head profusely, causing the feline to swing from side to side as it screeched like a stuck pig. Eventually I stopped when I realized that all had gone silent as everyone eyeballed my current situation. The guests had varying degrees of shock, horror, disbelief, and disgust across their faces. I had officially become the train wreck that everyone can't help but watch. Once they saw that I had become conscious of their stares, the place erupted in pandemonium. My mother rushed to the rescue and together we unhinged the cat from my jaw. I asked her how badly I was injured since I was fairly certain that at this point my face could only be identified via dental records. My mother assured me that I wasn't bleeding and everything was just fine. This calmed me down so I went inside to check on my battle wounds. When I got into the bathroom and turned on the light I concluded that my own mother had deceived me. The image I saw in the mirror was like something out of a gruesome slasher flick. Blood was spattered across one side of my face, and tears ran down the other.

After cleaning my puncture wound and rejoining the party, I received no sympathy. In fact, everyone was busy adding insult to injury, making sure the cat was okay and hadn't broken a nail on my face. They took their turns hassling me for messing with the animal in the first place, saying things like "face wounds help you build character" and "you got what was coming to you, young man" and even my grandma told me not to worry because my enormous head would continue to draw attention away from my face. Of course, she was on the sauce that day. Overall, no one seemed very concerned for my physical or emotional health. I tried to take comfort in the fact that all of the guests would leave that night and have nightmares of a boy flailing wildly with a cat stuck to his face.

Water Guns, and Other Things That Don't Normally Hurt People

I was raised in Ohio where the winters are long and cold and the summers are beautiful but come and go far too quickly. We had to take advantage of the heat while we could and one of my father's favorite ways to do this was by tasking my sister and me with outdoor manual labor. However, he also enjoyed a good water gun fight.

Back in the days before using a water gun was viewed as a sign that your son or daughter might grow up to be a gang member, hoodlum, or Charlton Heston, my father would regularly challenge his children to a good old H20 brawl. During one particularly hot summer, my sister and I loaded our bright yellow and green Super Soaker 3,000 water cannons and pumped them up for the oncoming battle, while my dad was elsewhere loading a couple of rickety plastic water pistols. We chased each other around the house and unloaded in a flurry of water blasts and prepubescent screams. The only way to really win in a water gun fight is to spray your opponent in the face until they submit. This is the key to victory as well as the only way to really deal any damage. This was also the first summer where the violence escalated.

As we chased my dad, who was completely out-gunned, into the front yard, the war waged its way up onto a wooden deck that stood roughly a foot or two off the ground. Running low on ammo and taking constant streams of water to the retinas, my father had to make a crucial decision: flee or fight. He decided that fleeing would allow him to get to the nearest water spigot to reload. His exit strategy was simple: shoot what little water was left in the guns at the offsprings' faces and run like hell.

While this process seemed good in theory, he forgot to factor in the deck we were standing on, which as I mentioned, was some feet off the ground. As he made his mad dash for freedom, he slipped off the edge and the ground quickly made contact with the majority of his face and chest region. Quickly rolling over, he threw up his hands in surrender, shielding him from the onslaught that we were delivering, and in between water blasts we were instructed to stop as he was possibly injured and that we should retrieve our mother immediately or we would regret ever being born. Now, I always thought myself to be a pretty clever kid and I had been fooled by this charade one too many times. In my mind there was no way that the fall he took could have subdued him and he was probably just "playing possum" or faking it, and I would prove it. I did what any kid would have done in that situation and continued to spray him in the face with my water gun.

In retrospect, I'm sure it looked downright brutal as I stood over the mangled mass that was my father, using a sort of advanced Chinese water torture on him. Through the gurgles I'm pretty sure I heard him begin to beg for his life and make peace for his trip into the afterlife, but in my mind this had to be part of the act. After several minutes I began to take his sobbing seriously and halted. My sister, wide-eyed at the no holds barred attack that I had just unleashed on my old man, ran to get my mother. I took off as well but in the opposite direction. I figured that if I got a head start, I just might live long enough to regret it.

Thankfully, the concussion that he received from the fall pretty much wiped out any memory of this event. Nowadays we can all look back on it and laugh. Well, everyone except for my father: He doesn't understand what's so funny.

Little League Baseball, and Other Things That Almost Killed Me

L ike most young boys growing up, I was coerced by the forces of evil, also known as my father, into participating in Little League Baseball. In retrospect, I'm surprised that I survived.

My baseball career started fairly young where both boys and girls were on the field together and an adult was brought in to pitch the ball underhanded to the children. This was likely a safety precaution to lower the chances of someone's being hurt. However, this logic was counteracted by the fact that the games were held at a baseball diamond nestled deep within the grounds of a local mental institution.

It wasn't enough that I had to worry about playing well and winning the game, but I also had to deal with the possibility that one of my teammates could be dragged off the field by the inhabitants of the loony bin. For whatever reason, most of the patients living there were allowed free roam of the place, and numerous times we were forced to stop our games while the guy who thought he could fly ran out into the middle of everything, shrieking at the top of his lungs. I didn't sleep much after those games.

The doctors in the white coats would soon race to the rescue, sedate him, and walk him back inside so that we could continue on. At the end of the game, it never mattered which team won or lost because everyone was too emotionally scarred to really care. I was never an outstanding baseball player and the only skill sets that I ever really developed in Little League were stealing bases and running from the crazies.

As we grew older, the girls graduated to playing softball while the boys upgraded to fast-pitch baseball where my peers were now the ones chucking a rock-hard, rubber-coated piece of cork at my face. This was the beginning of the end for me. The coaches got more serious and the testosterone levels were kicked up a notch. Suddenly the days of standing in the outfield daydreaming and hoping a psychopath didn't waylay me were a thing of the past.

Since I was quite small and fast I was always counted on to reach a base and then eventually score a point for the team. Even though gifted in speed and balance, I completely lacked the ability to hit the ball initially. This drove my coach mad. So much so in fact, that he once spent an entire practice teaching me how to bunt the ball in hopes that I could get on base and then begging me to retain the information until the next game. I was so terrible at batting that I had earned myself a sort of reputation. Each time that I got up to the plate, the pitcher would call his entire team to move in closer, knowing very well that if I hit the ball it would be a complete accident on my part. In order to amuse themselves, the pitchers of all the other teams decided that rather than pitch the ball to me, they would start throwing it *at* me, seeing if they could hit my rail thin frame and shatter me like a glass vase.

Since getting smacked with the ball equaled automatically getting a spot on first base, my coach was never happier and I was able to consistently score many points for the team. We won game after game when all I wanted was to lose so the season would be over. My lack of actual baseball skill paired with my uncanny ability to always be hit with a baseball at forty miles an hour netted me respect from the coach, respect from my team, and an MVP award at the end of the season. Of course, with all the bruises I was getting, I'm sure my schoolteachers assumed that my parents were mercilessly beating me at home.

Eventually I realized two things: the first was that maybe baseball wasn't for me, and second, I wanted to live to see the age of sixteen. Shortly after that I quit the team to go look for something a little less violent. I enrolled in Tae Kwon Do classes instead.

Birthday Spankings, and Other Violent Family Traditions

It was a tradition in my family that with every birthday that came to pass, the birthday boy or girl would receive not only cake and presents, but also a round of ritualistic birthday spankings. However, several years ago we had to put this custom to rest because too many family members were getting hurt.

It was impossible to enjoy one's birthday with the constant threat of inevitability lurking around every corner. Just when you thought everyone had forgotten about the spankings that year, you were tackled by a cousin and sat on by an uncle while your father subdued your hands, and Grandma pinned your arms to the floor. There's nothing quite like the feeling of getting jumped by your own family. In retrospect, I'm surprised they didn't steal my wallet in the process. I've never seen a group of people go from celebrators to lynch mob so quickly in my life. Once you were down and you had stopped clawing, biting, and screaming in a feeble attempt to escape, everyone would line up and the fun would commence, each member of the family giving you a number of spankings equal to your age. Even my great grandmother who was pushing ninety-five and hadn't walked in seven years would get up out of her wheelchair to join the festivities. It was a weird bonding experience that brought us closer as a family. So what if you couldn't sit down for the next week and half, as long as everyone had a good time.

As the years passed we saw lots of clever attempts to either diminish the pain of the spankings or avoid them altogether. I remember one year in particular when my sister thought it smart to stuff her pants full of toilet paper so that when she was eventually thrown to the floor and lovingly assaulted by twelve of her kin, maybe it wouldn't cause the bruises and welts normally acquired during the process. I'll tell you, there's something about a girl on a kitchen floor sobbing and screaming at the top of her lungs while family members rip bath tissue out of her pants with maniacal looks on their faces that really burns itself into your memory. Her birthday gifts that year included a pair of shoes, a gift card to her favorite store, and ultimate humiliation.

Another year, my aunt decided that she'd had enough of the tradition. She locked herself in a bedroom and barricaded the door. My father and my uncle spent a lot of time and energy breaking into the room only to find that she had escaped outside through a window. It was only a matter of time until she was dragged inside, kicking and screaming, thrown to the kitchen floor and the cycle repeated.

If memory serves, the final nail in the birthday spanking coffin came one year on my dad's birthday. As we ceremoniously attempted to clobber him to the floor, he put up a fight that we weren't prepared for. Failing to subdue him completely, my uncle jumped on his back in an attempt to take him down so the paddle party could begin. In a single heartbeat my father somehow channeled the spirit of Bruce Lee, flipped my uncle over his shoulder, and sent him sprawling face first into a nearby television set, his nose immediately becoming a geyser of blood. For the first time in as long as I can remember, we all stopped. Right then we were completely aware of just how real the situation had become.

Slightly ashamed of ourselves and also slightly disappointed about breaking the tradition, we decided to adopt a replacement activity for all future birthdays. It was something about putting candles on a cake, lighting them on fire, and then blowing them out. We found the concept foreign and not nearly as much fun, but we heard that that's how normal families do it.

Easter Egg Dyeing, and Other Holiday Activities Ruined by My Father

E aster was always an interesting time in my household. I use the word "interesting" to put a positive spin on the situation when deep down inside I wanted to write adjectives like "absurd," "frustrating," and "emotionally scarring."

You see, in my home, Easter was serious business, especially when it came to the traditional dyeing of hard-boiled eggs. For whatever reason, my father always became very militant during this holiday in what I assumed was an attempt to create the same "interesting" experience that he grew up with. It was the one holiday where he could really take charge and play dictator to our family.

The first order issued to my mother, my sister and me was to scour the earth and bring back eggs from the supermarket. Shortly thereafter, the kitchen became an assembly line of boiling ridiculous numbers of eggs and prepping them for what was to come. The second order of business was that we locate the correct egg dye for the big event. It couldn't be any ordinary egg dye. It had to be the coloring that came in tiny Victorian looking glass bottles and had a plastic rabbit's head for a stopper. According to him, all other dyes were sub-par and thoroughly un-American.

As the eggs finished boiling, my father would bring out a gigantic bowl reserved only for this particular day and event and would spend the next half an hour meticulously adding just the right amount of dye to the bowl of water. One by one, drops of red, green, yellow, and blue splashed into the bowl with surgical precision. He didn't believe in solid color eggs, so this preparation would provide us with multiple shades which would stain the shells with a second rate tie-dye effect. As he stooped over the basin, his eyes wide, he looked something like a mad scientist in a flannel shirt, his untamed chest hair spilling over the collar.

From there, the rest of us mere humans were to form a circle around the bowl and were given a specific tool which we would use to move the hard-boiled eggs from the table, into the bowl, and back out again. It wasn't a spoon, or a ladle, or any other tool of practicality. Instead, it was one of those wire contraptions that was bent all kinds of ways to cradle an egg, though it was so flimsy that it could barely support the weight. Egg dyeing isn't the most complex of processes and one would think that just dipping an egg into the dye would be enough. The Commander General, my father, would consider this a false statement. According to him we were to place the egg gently onto the dipping wire and enter it into the dye while moving our arms in a clockwise motion at a specific velocity that he had predetermined by calculating the time of day, multiplied by the speed of the earth's rotation, divided by the current alignment of the planets. It was an intense mathematical formula that he never shared with anyone.

After the egg dyeing orientation had ended, my family members would line up and take turns dyeing the eggs while my father closely supervised the entire process. When it was my turn, I would put the egg into the apparatus and slowly begin to lower it towards the bowl of colored water. Nine times out of ten my father would tell me to stop before the egg even broke the surface, and I would receive a lecture on how wrongly I was approaching the dyeing process. He would then throw around accusations that my family wasn't taking it seriously enough. If my second attempt to dye the egg still wasn't up to his standards, he would take it from me and do it himself. I was then sent to the back of the line.

With all the guidelines written out in the Easter egg dyeing policies and procedures manual, there was one rule that we weren't to break under any circumstances: Once the egg had entered the dye, we were not to lose control and drop it to the bottom of the bowl. For if the egg were accidentally separated from its transport device, then we would end up with an unacceptable drab gray Easter egg that would ruin the spirit of the holiday. Furthermore, whoever accidentally created one of these embarrassing abominations, had to be the one to eat it.

Each year, this exhaustive process ended one of two ways. Either we dyed all the eggs and kept our sanity, or one by one we boycotted his madness and left to do other things until my father was left in the room to finish dyeing the eggs alone. Which, in retrospect, was probably what he wanted all along.

Lawn Mowing, and Other Ridiculous Attempts to Build Character

I can very clearly recollect the first time I ever mowed the lawn at my father's request. I remember it because it was summer. The sun was bright, the weather was perfect, and I recall the amazing smell of the fresh-cut grass as it tickled my nose. Mainly, however, I remember it because it was also the very last time I ever mowed the lawn.

Throughout my youth, my father had me on a never-ending mission to build character. It was the reasoning he gave for every meaningless chore that was ever assigned to me. Why do I have to split wood? Because it builds character. Why do I have to pick up sticks in the woods? Because it builds character. Why do I have to build a Flux Capacitor? Come on, you've seen the pattern here. Because it builds character!

I managed to make it to the end of my senior year in high school before I was finally assigned the task of mowing the lawn. My father usually took charge of that because he never trusted anyone else to do it correctly. One day I guess he ran out of trivial things to occupy my time and decided to throw a real task my way. He hauled out the big red push-mower into the front yard and proceeded to show me how it was done.

Now, our front yard wasn't your average small, flat, fenced-in area. Instead, ours was quite large and included a steep hill and several obstacles, including trees, stumps, a wooden deck, and several flower beds. I was confused as to why I was going to take a trial run at mowing it because I was pretty certain that he didn't want any of the aforementioned things destroyed. His number one rule was that before I was allowed to mow the grass, I had to be able to turn the machine on. This was no simple mission that was completed with a power switch or the turn of a key. This particular mower was one that you had to prime, and then quickly and strongly pull the cord to start the engine turning. This was also my father's demented idea of a character-building rite of passage that I completely failed at. I've always been a small guy and to be completely honest, I'm fairly sure that my father had more muscles in his left arm than I did in my entire body. I primed the engine and yanked that cord as hard as I could.

When nothing happened, neither of us looked very surprised. My father demanded that I take another try at it while I reminded him of his rule about not being allowed to mow the lawn if I couldn't turn the mower on. Several more unsuccessful attempts later, my arm nearly ripped from the socket, he decided to start up the engine for me since we were now running out of daylight. Once we got the mower into motion, my father headed inside, leaving me to tend the yard. Everything was going smoothly until I got to the small hill. I approached it cautiously, not wanting to send the mower careening into the nearby flowerbeds. As I started down, I gained more momentum than I expected and before I knew it I was being dragged down the hill behind the mower.

Before I carried out any chore assigned by my father, he would give a long-winded explanation of the job and how to do it correctly. I always expected his instructional seminars to be followed by a written exam. Luckily, I had paid attention during Lawn Mower 101 and remembered that if I let go of the handle, there was a mechanism that would kill the engine. I let go of the handle and slammed to the ground while the mower traveled a few more feet before coming to a stop. Hearing the engine turn off, my father emerged from the house to investigate. When I explained to him my tale of woe about not being strong enough to control the thing, he did exactly what he always did-- sent me inside and did the job himself.

After several mower-free months had passed, he decided out of the blue that it was time for me to build more character. This time he wanted to throw a real challenge my way. Moments later I had a chainsaw in my hands. I took a look at the primer and the pull cord and knew right then that someone was probably going to get hurt.

Childhood Fads, and Other Ways to Poorly Spend Your Hard-Earned Money

Everyone had those things that they collected growing up. In retrospect, I'm sure that most of these items were downright ridiculous but that didn't stop us from investing hundreds of dollars in them when perhaps the time would have been better spent shoveling our life savings into a big burlap sack, dragging it out to the middle of a field and setting it ablaze. I am by no means an exception to this rule. I went through many phases growing up, but I also had the ability to see when one of my fads had run its course and it was time to move on to the next.

It all started with my collection of hats. More specifically, they were of the baseball cap variety with the classic brim, and the puzzle-like dots and holes fastener in the back that I never became very adept at manipulating. There's a good chunk of my life where friends and family never saw the top of my head. For years and years I would find and purchase these hats, receive them as gifts, or I would get hand-me-down caps from my friends, family, and complete strangers, which admittedly was a little strange, but went unquestioned. What started as just a ball cap or two quickly turned into a rampant collection that I did not have the space for. I remember having stacks of hats layered onto each of my bedposts, and a cache of caps stashed underneath my bed, hidden away like the black sheep of the family that you convince to stay locked up in the guest room during Thanksgiving. Like most people, I had my favorite hats, so a good ninety percent of them probably went unworn. Over time I started accumulating hats from various baseball teams and came to a self-realization that I had no interest in sports, and more importantly, had never shown any interest in them at any point throughout my youth. By the end of this phase I found myself knee-deep in numerous sports-related head coverings, the teams of which I couldn't name with a gun to my head. I realized that it was time to move on with life.

I had decided that maybe hats were far too decadent for my characteristics and became interested in collecting something a little more naturalistic. So of course, that led me to amass rocks instead. This trend made more sense because the majority of interesting looking stones that I would come across were found outside and thus free for the taking. Because of my enthusiasm for stones, I remember celebrating a Christmas where the majority of my gifts were rock themed. I received a guidebook to gemstones, a handful of colorful pebbles that were from "an exotic location," which I later discovered to be a park in Cleveland, as well as a rock tumbler. If you're unfamiliar with a rock tumbler, it's essentially a canister that you load up with stones and hook to a motor that rolls them around to smooth them out. This process lasts about as long as it takes the Moon to make a complete orbit around the Earth, all while emitting a noise similar to that of a wounded raccoon swimming in Tabasco sauce while engulfed in flames. There's a reason that this gift was never marketed as "fun for the whole family." Days later, If you remembered to return to the rock tumbler after it had finished its cycle, then you were rewarded with polished stones that could be glued to the accompanying earring and key chain accessories. I obviously don't have to go into detail on what gifts my family members received from me on the ensuing holidays. As time wore on, I realized that much like the hats, I was quickly running out of practical places to stash piles of rocks, and the fact that my grandmother would surprise me with a bag of random bedrock whenever she visited was not helping. It didn't take long to identify that the "gift" of "interesting rocks" was actually just gravel from the driveway of my own home. I moved on with life.

One of the final phases I went through was when I began collecting pencils. This phase was kicked off when my grandmother donated a large box of pencils from all over the world and from different time periods. Much like myself, she was running out of room in her basement and pawned them off on me as a special gift. The next holiday was then pencil themed and much like my previous interests, the pencil pile quickly grew out of control and soon I was sitting upon boxes of unused pencils that I would not allow my friends or family to sharpen, completely believing that this would ruin the monetary value that this collection would eventually incur after sitting through several ice ages, three apocalyptic asteroid collisions with Earth, and the rapture itself. Having gifted me with every interesting pencil ever manufactured in the history of the world, my family began to deliver packs of boring yellow number two pencils. That winter I'm pretty sure we burned the entire collection to stay warm, and I moved on with life.

Power Outages, and Other Catastrophes My Father May Have Premeditated

My father isn't someone who believes in the luxuries of the modern world. He's obsessed with history and I'm sure that deep down he wishes he had been born a hundred years earlier so he could rub elbows with Civil War generals and assassinate anyone who may have dreamt up an idea that could eventually lead to the creation of a home computing device. In our home, CD players, video games that connected to the television set, computers, and air conditioning were all outlawed. He's a man who enjoys the simple things in life like water and fire. Anything else was considered excessive.

When not working, my father spent his time lurking in the shadows, waiting to catch one of his children doing something wrong. If you were caught leaving a room without turning off the light behind you, then my father would appear out of nowhere to sit you down and lecture about the importance of saving energy, ensuring that if he had his way then we wouldn't even have lights in the first place. His logic dictated that if it was too dark to see, then we didn't need to be doing anything. Our family was nearly torn apart on several occasions by arguments started when the refrigerator door was open for what he deemed as "too long."

Power outages, seen by many as a giant hassle and inconvenience, were my father's favorite thing in the world. The moment the house went black, he went skipping to the closet, most likely with a giant smile on his face, to fish out the oil lamps which he greeted as though they were long lost relatives. They were lit and strategically placed about the living room to provide a dim glow that still did not allow for you to see your hand in front of your face. My sister's first instinct would be to haul out a flashlight, but she was quickly chastised and told to save the batteries for a "real emergency." The family was gathered together in one room to experience what it would be like to live in the "olden times." I humored him and pretended that I was back in the 1800's. As I looked around the 1800's room I could almost see my sister developing eyestrain while playing her Game Boy in the shadows and I watched my mother attempt to do the Sunday crossword puzzle by candlelight while having to stop every few seconds to ensure the newspaper didn't get too close to the flame and catch fire. This scene didn't seem historically accurate. During some of the longer evenings that we spent in the Dark Ages, I often suspected that my father had actually sneaked out back and cut the power of his own accord.

My mother was the opposite of my dad. She enjoyed new technologies that made our lives simpler and more efficient. Whenever she would use the hard-earned washing machine, you could almost smell my father disapproving of the fact that she wasn't down on her hands and knees with a basin and washboard appreciating "the way things used to be." He would sneer at the oven, disappointed that it wasn't an open fire, and he would scoff at the television set, wishing that it were an old transistor radio that only received one station and only picked up reception while the sun was out.

The rest of my family would often conspire on how to get new technologies into the home under my father's watchful eye. More often than not, if we painted a picture of how it would benefit him, he would cave and we would be willing to continue living there. These charges had to be led by my mother, for if my sister and I challenged him, we had no hopes of winning. My sister's teenage cries for a car went unheard and instead she was given a horse. Practicality was never my father's strong suit. I opted to take a more aggressive approach and smuggled technology into the house like some sort of criminal. My first compact disc player came home in the bottom of my school bag after a nefarious parking lot bartering session with a classmate. Scared that my father would discover the contraband, it would only come out at night after he was asleep.

Somewhere along the line, my mother managed to talk the boss into allowing a computer into the home. Not only would it make her professional job easier, but also would allow the rest of us to feel like we were living in the twentieth century. When the computer arrived, Dad wanted nothing to do with it and vowed before all of us never to touch it. He argued that he had his typewriter and that would do him just fine. As time wore on, I would catch him having stare downs with the computer, a silent argument raging between the two of them. After several months he began making attempts to learn how to use it and after he was shown that word processing would allow him to drop typewriter ribbon from his monthly budget, he was sold. The day I showed him how to run Internet searches for Civil War information and antiques, he joined the rest of us in wondering how he had ever lived without it.

My father has a reputation for being a stubborn man, but he seems to be loosening up in his old age. A year or so ago I received an exuberant phone call from my mother. She couldn't wait to give me the exciting news that after twenty-five years she had managed to talk him into getting an air conditioner... if only for one room of the house. We've learned to cherish the small victories.

Splitting Wood, and Other Chores I Never Volunteered For

Ohio summers are exceptionally hot and the winters are downright frigid. The household where I grew up didn't have air conditioning of any kind, so in order to keep cool in the summer, my father allowed the rest of the family to haul the box fans out of storage. To save on electricity costs we were only to run them at night and spent the daytime poised in front of open windows, bargaining with a greater power that we would never do anything bad again in exchange for a stiff breeze. In the winter we would run the old furnace that lived in our basement and was roughly the size of the house itself. In order to operate efficiently, it needed to be loaded up with firewood every ten to fifteen seconds. My father would spend the entire year gearing up for the cold weather, well aware of the furnace's eating habits, and months were spent collecting firewood whenever possible, all of it coming from fallen trees from the woods we lived in.

This lumber couldn't go straight from the woods to its fiery doom, but instead needed to be split in order to fit through the furnace door. This was one of the chores that my father recruited me for, assuring me that it would help to build character. Luckily, he didn't just throw me an axe and send me to the chopping block, as one in my situation would expect, but instead he would rent a rather low-tech wood splitter from a local farming store to help get the job done.

The wood splitter was a gas-powered machine with a mechanical arm that would push logs into a wicked blade at extremely slow speeds. My job was to sit on an upended piece of wood and throw the lever back and forth to make the arm go forward or retract while my father loaded the logs onto the track and then stacked the split pieces. This lever would vibrate uncontrollably with the heave of the engine block and my arm and shoulder would become uncomfortably numb after just twenty minutes into the job.

Much like the lawnmower and his favorite chainsaw, the wood splitter would only come to life with a superhuman yank of the pull starter. My father didn't believe in simple on-off switches and maintained that all heavy machinery should only start by the power of a man's arm. Since I was a rather small fellow, also known in some countries as a weakling, I lacked the power of this mythical man's arm that he spoke of. Because of my physical shortcomings, my father was elected to start the machine. One of his favorite things to preach was that a person should always work smarter and not harder, but when I would argue this motto versus the impossible pull starter, the hypocrite would tell me to man up and not question his elders. The starting apparatus caused me so much stress that I often had nightmares that I would wake up to find the power buttons of the blender, microwave oven, and television remote mysteriously replaced with pull starters.

Over the course of the long hours that it would take to split our way through the pile of future warmth, my goal was always to find some way to make the process interesting for myself. I would try to speculate on what types of bugs we might find buried deep within the pieces of wood. I always saw new and exciting species of ants, spiders, and grubs scramble frantically as their former homes were torn apart by a massive blade. They would scurry in different directions, but more often than not, they'd run right towards my father who would have to take an intermission from splitting in order to pound the attackers into dust with the closest log.

While waiting for its day to be halved, the wood had sat outside being exposed to different temperatures and causing pressure to build up inside some of the pieces. The second that those logs hit the blade, they would explode into several hundred pieces, rocketing timber shards towards our faces like shrapnel. It was nature's version of Russian roulette, so I spent a lot of time wondering which piece might try to end our lives. Another situation we'd encounter from time to time would be when my dad became a little overzealous and wanted to split a tree trunk that was clearly too thick to be dismembered in this fashion. As predicted, the wood became stuck on the end of the blade, not budging and sometimes stalling out the engine. For these exact moments he kept a sledgehammer nearby that he would use to free the wood in order to give it another try. This could take several quick taps or several long hours, depending on the initial hit of the mechanical arm.

By the time we'd reached the end of our session, we had a neatly stacked pile of split logs. I'd be ready to head inside to move on with my life and somewhere underneath the pile of bugs and kindling my father celebrated the victory in his own way. Then we'd walk back toward the house, both of us feeling a great sense of accomplishment. My dad would be dripping with sweat from handling all of the heavy lifting while I walked beside him, my comatose arm swinging in the breeze.

Chapter 3:
Workin' for the Man or Woman --
The Politically Correct Way to Title a
Chapter About the Corporate World

Three Handshakes That You Should Never Give or Receive

My job requires me to shake a lot of hands, both in a day-to-day setting and while conducting job interviews. I've spent a lot of time wondering why the handshake has been reinvented by new groups of people over the last few years as it has morphed from something simple, classic, and elegant into a knuckle pounding, hand slapping, chest bumping display of aggression, but the reasoning has become crystal clear: some people just suck at the traditional style.

I was brought up with the understanding that a good handshake was firm, solid, and involved eye contact. Apparently the memo that went out to the rest of the world was not written legibly. I want to illustrate three handshakes that you should watch out for whenever you are meeting someone for the first time. I have learned these techniques through years and years of experience. This is real world stuff. They don't teach you this in college, so pay attention.

The first way not to shake hands is executed by receiving someone's hand in yours and proceeding to squeeze it tightly, hurting the other party as if they were responsible for a past death in your family, or your adoption as a child. Most people will not interpret this as a friendly greeting and more often than not the message conveyed is something akin to "I'll be waiting for you tonight in the parking lot. Be there!"

If you're applying for a job, then this handshake tells your potential employer that you are a jerk, and if you're meeting your girlfriend's father, it tells him that his daughter isn't really serious about the relationship. This method is commonly referred to as the "Trash Compactor" and is regularly employed by tough guys, dudes with tribal tattoos, and people who are overcompensating for something that will likely be found out later during a drunken birthday meltdown.

The next handshake that I hate receiving is called the "Finger Squeeze." It occurs as someone puts their hand in yours, but you go for the squeeze just a moment too soon and end up grabbing just four fingers and an awkward moment. Unlike the Trash Compactor, which is mostly uncomfortable for the receiver, this handshake is uncomfortable for both parties, especially if the required eye contact is in place. There's not much you can do to salvage this greeting and it's best to just let it die and look at absolutely anything else in the vicinity. If you're applying for a job, it tells your future boss that you will act awkward under pressure, and if you're meeting a Colombian drug lord, it tells them that there's no way that you're going to successfully smuggle the eight pounds of smack back into the States in your suitcase. People who are antisocial, have large hands, or bad eyesight usually use method two.

Lastly, the worst possible handshake you can give anyone, ever, at any time is known at most companies as the "Dead Fish." This is where someone takes your hand in his or hers and suddenly yours becomes a passenger. There is no squeeze or shake and you are simply along for the ride. This conveys no power, no confidence, and possibly a lack of hand tendons. If you present the dead fish, you should not be surprised if someone takes your limp hand and begins hitting you with it. You should not call for help, as this will only make it worse. At a job interview, this handshake will be seen as weak and uninterested, while on a first date, this shake gets you a one-way ticket to the Friend Zone. Permanently. Children or people in comas usually prefer this style of handshake.

In closing, I would ask that everyone familiarize themselves with the correct way to shake hands or you might put yourself in a bad situation before you even get to exchanging names. It requires a firm grip, mutual eye contact, and no more then two pumps. Anything more than two pumps will tell the other person that you are loosening up their arm and might quite possibly try to steal it later for a meal or for auction on the black market. Now get out there and greet the world. Correctly.

The Lamborghini of Office Chairs

I hate to be the bearer of bad news and it pains me to be so brutally honest, but occasionally things just have to be said in order to clear the air. Sometimes thoughts and emotions are just too heavy to be kept inside and if you don't let them out, you feel as if you might explode. So here I am to relieve myself of the burden and clear my conscience once and for all. I regret to inform you, the reader, that my office chair at work is just entirely too comfortable for my own good.

About a year ago, a new manager was brought into my department and for his very first order of business he suggested not that we balance the department's budget, not that we set out to double our overall effectiveness, and not that we increase our overall productivity, but instead he suggested that we celebrate his arrival by going out and buying new chairs for the management staff. This was a welcome idea at the time, as the chair that I had spent three years sitting in resembled something similar to a bucket with wheels.

Off we went, he and I, ultimately arriving at a local office supply store. With stars in our eyes we began the enthusiastic search for the ideal chair. We then spent the next three hours sitting in hundreds of office chairs of every color, shape, and size, test-driving each one in the search of the seat in which we would achieve maximum comfort and style. The elderly store employee in charge of the furniture section had a hard time keeping up with us as we youthfully darted from chair to chair occasionally hollering feedback to each other as we raced up and down the rows. Shouts of "Does that one feel good?" and "Oh dude, you have to try this one!" could be heard as far away as the printer ink aisle. The store employee, mildly confused at seeing two guys who were just way too into office furniture, had eventually winded himself by chasing us about the warehouse and let us know where we could find him if we needed assistance. Exhaustedly he sat down on a nearby table, likely preparing himself for the afterlife.

Just when we thought we'd seen everything, we spotted a heavenly glow surrounding a lonesome high back leather chair across the room. At last we had found it. The one. The Lamborghini of office chairs. We approached it slowly, as if it were a mythical creature that might spook and run for cover if we moved too quickly. As we came upon it, the glow engulfed us. We may as well have just found the Ark of the Covenant. My boss invited me to sit first and give my thoughts. I lowered myself onto the lush leather and immediately sank deeply into it, the chair hitting me in all the right places. The only feedback I could offer up was a contented sigh. After several moments I wrestled myself away from its grasp so he could give it a try. He took a deep breath, sat down, and instantaneously fell asleep.

We decided right then and there that the chair was pure evil and therefore we had to have it. The old store employee stopped walking towards the light long enough to locate two more of the chairs in the back. After paying up we returned to the office with chairs in tow and wide smiles on our faces.

A year later, I still enjoy the never-ending comfort that the chair provides. Each day it's there to give me a big leather hug and cradle me while I sit. Lately, I've even been entertaining the notion that I just might finally get around to doing some actual work.

Couples Therapy

Exactly one floor above the office where I work there is a
therapist who counsels couples. Based on what I see and
hear as these patients come and go, this doctor just might be to
blame for the climbing divorce rates.

Often times I get to see patients arrive for their
appointments and they never fail to amuse. They show up,
meet by the staircase leading to the counselor's office and then
proceed to head in for their session. Most times the couples
arrive in separate cars and spend five minutes bickering with
one another in the parking lot before heading inside for round
number two. Other times the gloves stay on and they
rendezvous in complete silence. For these moments I take the
liberty of making up my own assumptions about them and their
current situation. It might sound cruel and superfluous, but
then, so was high school.

The very first couple I witnessed, Jack and Joan (these
names are, of course, made up), met at the stairs and Joan
proceeded to yell at Jack at high volumes because the previous
night he had gone to a bar after work and arrived home an hour
later than usual. This led Joan to assume that he had hooked up
with approximately seventeen high school cheerleaders over
the course of that hour. Jack was adamant about calming her
down since they were out in public and I was standing
awkwardly a mere ten feet away, but that only forced Joan to
continue her slander to both Jack and everyone else within

earshot. I saw this couple more than anyone else. They also argued more than anyone else. They eventually stopped showing up altogether and I had to assume that Jack had probably taken his own life from having to deal with her.

Another couple I witnessed was Rick and Robin (again, these are false names). They were a couple that arrived in silence and left in silence, each taking their own vehicle to their own destinations, which I'm guessing were not the same place. This was another one of those times when I had to make up a reason for their needing counseling. Since Rick was short and fat with a bad case of hair loss, I assumed that he probably wasn't hooking up with many cheerleaders these days. Robin was several years younger, stern looking, and always dressed like she was going to a funeral. Perhaps in the end, she was. From what I could gather, Robin was middle management at a semi-successful company and was weary from being passed over for every promotion. In her eyes, she would never fully succeed in the "man's world" that is software engineering. She was a feminist who owned sixteen cats and had an insatiable lust for "Cherry Garcia" ice cream. Rick was a narcoleptic hypochondriac with an insatiable lust for Big Mac's. As irony would have it, the trigger for his narcolepsy was cats. You can just see the drama unfolding in your mind.

Sure, there have been other couples and other stories and I really wish that I had the heart to tell the tale about Max the mail man and Megan the Dog Trainer, or even Sarah the vegetarian and Seth the butcher. They were good couples.

Were.

Saving The Day
with Vague Answers

Sometimes in life the less we say, the bigger impact it has upon those around us. I didn't really comprehend the previous statement until several years deep into my experience as a manager at work. At my office job I've begun to notice how a casual remark can turn the tide of my department's future. Let me illustrate.

My job obligates me to sit through a lot of meetings. We have meetings in the morning, meetings in the afternoon, meetings during lunch and meetings right before the end of the day. Often times we have meetings to plan out the meetings we will have in the future and then have post-meetings to recap the events that took place within those meetings. Nine times out of ten these meetings are important and determine future practices and protocols that I need to be familiar with in order to help manage them; however, there are the occasions when a meeting is so extremely dull in nature, that instead of paying attention to the ideas and details being thrown out around me, I will drift off and occasionally do long division in my head just to pass the time. After I've spent a chunk of time drifting and I have solved the world's biggest problems and pondered my future two or three times over, I will return to my body in time to hope that the meeting doesn't end right as my leg is falling asleep for the eighth time that hour. Let me tell you, nothing is more embarrassing and awkward than walking out of a meeting while dragging a dead limb behind you.

I normally do very well controlling my zoning. I went to high school and college, thus giving me years of experience in this field. If I am led to believe that my participation will be needed at any point in one of these meetings, then I will stay focused and contribute as necessary. The trouble comes during those times when I have resigned myself to the fact that my input will not be needed and I am just filling a seat. That opens the doorway to begin the zoning out process. Then it happens: suddenly and without warning I am thrust into the midst of the conversation by someone asking me a question. I am immediately snapped back into my body to realize that a.) I have no idea what the question was, and b.) I now have five sets of eyes staring at me intently, waiting on pins and needles for an important answer. It's during these situations where my vague answers can save the day.

My vague answers come in three forms: "agreement," "deep thought," and "confident indifference." All three of these formats have saved me at one point or another. Often times when the question is asked, the first thing I will do is quickly scan my memory banks and attempt to identify the last person whose voice I heard while I was zoning out. If I am able to do this quickly enough, then I can produce a response to let everyone know that "I really agree with what Jim said." This causes everyone to sit silently for a moment before the heads start nodding and the discussion continues. When I go with deep thought, I furrow my brow, put my chin onto my fist and let out a "Hmm" that lets everyone around me know that I am pondering the question. Eventually they will tire of the silence and announce that maybe it's smart to rethink the situation. Lastly, there are the times where I snap out of my daydream to find myself armed with no prior knowledge of the conversation that is in progress. In these tough situations I will sit back, make eye contact with each individual in the room and give them a very confident yet indifferent, "Sure!"

It's not uncommon for my managers to tell me after these meetings how much they respect my ability to make quick decisions under pressure and that if I hadn't been in that particular meeting, then there's no way they would have reached the conclusion I provided. After these meetings, all I'm usually thinking about is how long division is easier with a calculator.

Awkward House Shopping

A while back I got a new boss at work. I say that like it was some sort of Christmas present. It's not that he was wrapped up with a bow by upper management, but I'm really not sure how else to word it. He was hired from an outside company to get my department on track and he's an all-around super nice fellow whom I get along with very well. All good managers feel that it's important to get to know those with whom they will be working on a daily basis and he felt no different. One day on our lunch break, he convinced me to go house shopping with him since he was looking for a new place to live. We justified doing this on the clock by dubbing it a "Team Building Exercise." I got into his car and he drove us straight to the ritziest, most Republican part of town to look at houses that I can only describe as "out of my league."

We waltzed our way into one of the bigger properties to have a look around and were immediately greeted by a cordial real estate agent who was eager to show us the house. We went through the kitchen and the agent asked us if we liked to cook. My boss said that out of the two of us, he was probably the better cook and I announced that I have enough trouble working a microwave. We laughed and continued into the living room where the realtor asked if we enjoyed relaxing and watching the game. My boss said he never misses a big sporting event and I asked which sport "the game" referred to. I was being quite serious but we all laughed again. It wasn't until we headed upstairs into the master bedroom where the agent proclaimed, "You see guys? There would be plenty of room for both of you in here" that I realized he had the wrong idea all along. An awkward silence filled the room, and nobody laughed.

That's Probably a Health Code Violation

For the males who work in my office, bathroom time is an awkward time as the men's restroom is in a rather strange location. Unlike the lady's room, which is tucked away in a quiet and peaceful corner, far, far away from the hardships of the world, ours is in the kitchen. Yes, the kitchen. It's right smack in the middle of the area where all the employees from the entire building go to take their breaks, eat their lunches and have water cooler talk about which color of Post-It notes is superior.

Every man in the department learns quickly that he has to master the art of managing his restroom time effectively because if he doesn't go early on in the day, then he runs the risk of that super-large mega Starbucks coffee kicking in right when the all-female financial department sits down for their noontime lunch.

Before you know it, there you are, stuck in a single-toilet bathroom doing your business with an audience of thirteen to twenty gals who can clearly hear every stir, noise, and grunt through the paper-thin walls. The only thing worse than having your co-workers hear your most private of moments is then having to exit the restroom into a roomful of people who do everything in their power to avoid making eye contact with you as you do the walk of shame past them all.

You might be wondering if having a restroom in a kitchen is a health code violation. I'm no health inspector, but

I'm pretty sure it is. It also brings a new meaning to the old phrase "Don't poop where you eat." It all makes so much sense now.

Student, Meet Karma. Karma, Student.

I'm a firm believer in the cosmic principle according to which each person is rewarded or punished in one incarnation according to that person's deeds in the previous incarnation. However, in my opinion, nothing is better-- and not to mention funnier-- than instant karma.

I work at a university that on a daily basis has over five thousand students on campus. Now, take into consideration that each of these students has one car and drives it to class each day. Not only is that five thousand people who do not understand the concept of carpooling, but that's approximately four thousand students who won't be able to find a parking spot in the same zip code as the school. As you may imagine, this creates a bit of a problem.

In the office where I work, we have a small employee parking lot; however, the students think they are quite clever and if they are running late for class and all of the parking spots are full, they will sneak into our lot, park, and sprint off to class in hopes of not being seen and subsequently hunted down like wounded animals. Knowing how this creates a giant hassle for employees, we are asked to report violators to security so that their vehicles can be ticketed, towed, or have girlish stickers of Strawberry Shortcake and Rainbow Brite affixed to highly visible places (if we decide to take matters into our own hands). I understand how it may seem a bit callous to do this to people who are thousands upon thousands of dollars deep in student loans, but hey, no one said college would be easy.

Employees have small university tags, which hang from the rear-view mirror of their cars to indicate that they work for the school. Students are assigned giant neon stickers roughly the size of Kansas that are used to mark their vehicles. It's quite easy to spot a car or truck that doesn't belong. It's a lot like trying to hide an obese person somewhere in an Ethiopian village.

One day as I was returning to work from lunch I was unable to find parking in our lot. I circled around several times and saw car after car emblazoned with the neon orange student sticker taking up residence in our precious spaces. Eventually I gave up hope and was forced to find an empty spot on the outer limits of campus. I then started the long walk to my office under a hot Florida sun.

As I got closer to civilization, I noticed that classes were over and hordes of students were exiting the nearby classrooms to go home and study. And by "go home and study" I mean, "form a drum circle" or "play hacky sack."

I spotted two male students who strolled right from their class into our lot while walking and talking, looking as though they didn't have a care in the world and completely oblivious to the fact that I had essentially just walked through a desert due to their illegal parking schemes. They were laughing and high-fiving and having a great old time. Not only did they have the audacity to park in our sacred lot, but also had the nerve to stand together and chitchat once they had reached their vehicles. I was definitely in the mood for some revenge.

After wiping the sweat from my eyes, I could see that they were parked directly across from one another in the lot, the main driveway running between their cars. If I was quick about it, then I could get both of their license plate numbers to report to security before they knew what was happening. At that point my plan began to crumble, however, as they spotted the employee badge around my neck from a distance and bolted for their respective driver's seats. In their haste to get away, they fired up their engines, threw it in reverse and simultaneously backed out of the parking spots, their cars slamming right into one another. Before I had time to react, the two friends were out of their vehicles yelling at each other at the top of their lungs. Security was on the scene in a matter of moments and ticketed both drivers. I guess it's always best to remember that what goes around comes around… and sometimes it's in the form of your best friend's Toyota.

Job Postings for People with Overactive Bladders

L ooking for a new job? Having problems with constant urination? Is it preventing you from getting your work done on a daily basis? Are you starting to fear for your job? If so, imagine a world where you can get the hours you need, the schedule you want, and the ability to use that overactive bladder to your advantage. Put down the Detrol pills, stash away those adult diapers, and look into one of these exciting job postings that I have compiled for your viewing pleasure. I have scoured the Internet to bring you these exciting career opportunities that you may have never considered, yet you could be the perfect candidate for.

This interesting career option was found on careerbuilder.com

FIREFIGHTERS NEEDED

Do you like helping people? If so, you should consider an exciting career in firefighting. In this fast- paced and competitive discipline, you will have to respond to emergency calls, get to the scene quickly and safely, and deal with snuffing out anything that happens to be on fire. You may also be responsible for operating the truck siren, which we hear is a lot of fun. As a candidate with an overactive bladder, you may find yourself moving up quickly through the ranks from firefighter to lieutenant before you know it. It will be important that you are out on the front lines should the fire truck exhaust its water supply, if technical problems occur, or just in case some jerk's station wagon is parked in front of the closest hydrant. Even if these situations present themselves, it will be comforting to all of those in your squad to know that they can depend on your overactive bladder to put out the blaze. Applicants should drink lots of fluids, and not break the seal until the appropriate time. Training classes beginning soon, no experience necessary. Apply now!

I located the following posting on the ever-popular craigslist.org

IMMEDIATE OPENINGS AVAILABLE
IN MEDICAL FIELD

Hospitals are busy places and you could be one step away from helping someone who is in pain. Now more than ever coastal towns across America are facing an epidemic of jellyfish attacks. In the last month alone there has been a massive influx of jellyfish returning to the Atlantic and Pacific from Asia and Australia as they prepare for the warm waters of the summer months and since they heard that George W. Bush was no longer in office. While we are appreciative of the sudden wildlife boom, we are not all happy about them assaulting locals and beach goers in the tourist regions. We're looking for well-qualified individuals with overactive bladders to be standing by in our emergency rooms to be prepared for these attacks. It's well-known scientific fact that urine neutralizes the venom of the jellyfish, helping to relieve the pain and swelling until anti-venom can be injected or until that particular body part can be chopped off. The ideal applicant should be experienced urinating on different objects. On busy days you may be required to carry a water bottle and balance the fine line between a full bladder and water intoxication. Flexible hours, benefits, fast paced environment. R. Kelly need not apply.

And finally, this interesting job choice is directly from the job board on NASA.com:

WORK FOR NASA

Do you have an interest in the space program? Have you ever wanted to be an astronaut? Are you hoping to one day become a rocket scientist in one of our laboratories? If so, please stay in school and go study. If you're still reading this, then we at the National Aeronautics and Space Administration (NASA) are seeking self-motivated males and females with overactive bladders to contribute urine to our Orion Program. As you may have read, we have spent years developing a urine recycler to be installed on the International Space Station sometime in the next decade. This will convert the crew members' urine into clean, drinkable water and make the world a greener place. We've spent around thirty billion in tax dollars on this thing and we are still working out some kinks, namely that whole converting urine into water part. We've already hosted a handful of urine drives at various places around the United States, and you have to understand how embarrassing that was. We've called in all our favors and have hassled our family members enough. Position is full time with full benefits and offers lots of overtime. No experience necessary. We'll pretty much take anyone. We're desperate. Please, we need your pee.

Good luck on your job hunt. I wish you much success. *
Remember, your overactive bladder should not keep you from doing something you love. **

*None of these job postings are real. Please do not pursue them.
**But seriously, you should stick to taking prescribed medications and wearing adult diapers in the interim.

Chapter 4:
Cat Tales

Cats Vote, Decide That Closed Doors Offend Them

I live with two cats that have apparently, unbeknownst to me, gotten together and voted on a major issue. The polls are closed, the results are in, and they have decided that closed doors now offend them.

Sure, we all know that cats are curious creatures, but mine are getting to the point at which curiosity has taken a back seat to being antisocial and downright rude. They play the common cat games like the "Wake Up" competition, when, as I'm peacefully asleep, they take turns jumping high into the air and landing on my face to see who can wake me up so I will give them food. They also enjoy the game where they lie flat on their backs and put their bellies into the air, and each time I make an attempt to pat their soft undersides, they dig their claws deep into my arm and attempt to separate the flesh from the bone. I have affectionately come to refer to this one as the "Furry Bear Trap" game. They also hold the famous "Giant Killer" contest daily which occurs as I'm walking anywhere in my apartment. They scamper in front of my legs, causing me to fall and face plant into whatever furniture is closest. They especially like to play this game when I'm carrying piping hot coffee.

A few days ago the cats adopted a new game without telling me. I like to think that in their minds they're going to call it the "How Dare You Close the Door" game. Each morning as I lock myself away in the bathroom and prepare for the workday ahead, I will try to round them up and stick them inside with me so everyone is happy. However, if they're sleeping, or unable to be located, it's not going to stop me from getting to work on time. The other day I found myself in the shower, fighting to stay awake, when out of nowhere something hit the closed door with power reminiscent of an atomic bomb. I paused, not quite sure what had happened and stood perplexed as soap trickled into my eyes. Assuming that I had imagined the noise in my pre-coffee mental state, I continued with the shower, when moments later there was another slam on the door, louder than the first. At this point I told myself that the only logical explanation was that someone had broken into my apartment and was now shooting cannon balls at the bathroom door. Before I had time to take any type of safety precautions, such as tying the soap and shampoo bottles together like some type of shower nunchucks, there was another extremely loud bang on the door and it came flying open, slamming against the wall. I threw open the shower curtain and grabbed a loofah sponge for self-defense, but was greeted not by a burglar or a hooligan, but with the angry meows of two felines. They had won the new game.

Spray Bottles: Punishing Cats Since 1947

My girlfriend has a secret weapon in the never-ending battle with our cats. It's not catnip, nor a special toy, and it's not a harsh verbal projection that hits a specific frequency in their hearing range causing them pain. It's a simple spray bottle.

As of late, the number of plastic spray bottles in our apartment has begun to rival the number of drinking glasses available. It's not that we have decided to take up collecting them as an offbeat hobby, or are anticipating a world shortage, but rather we have been drafted as soldiers in a war against our cats.

In addition to doing anything in their power to force their way through closed doors, one of the cats has also made it very clear that she despises the Venetian window blinds. She likes to paw them out of the way so that she can see the outside world and, in doing so, makes a large racket similar to that of a drunk two year old wielding a chainsaw in a hen house. As with most bad feline habits, her disdain is usually at its worst while we are trying to sleep. It's gotten to the point where as soon as the cat starts to fuss with the window, my girlfriend, regardless of how deep into her slumber she is, will sit straight up, grab the spray bottle and unleash on the cat as if she were firing an AK-47. This sends the beast into a rampage and she darts into the living room, destroying anything in her path.

A few mornings ago I awoke for an early shift at work and noticed more light than usual pouring in through the window. I pulled back the curtain and was greeted by a set of maimed blinds. The slats were bent and broken so I went about meagerly attempting to fix them. The sound generated as I tried to reposition the slats created a noise eerily similar to that of the cat trying to paw its way out to freedom. Out of the corner of my eye, I saw a shape rise up from the bed and before I knew it, a barrage of spray bottle fire was raining down upon me.

In between ducking for cover and experiencing Vietnam-esque flashbacks of water gun fights with my father, I realized how viable a weapon the spray bottle truly was, and as I rampaged through my home destroying anything in my path, I knew how the cat felt. There's something enlightening about an ice-cold spear of liquid striking you repeatedly that really makes you consider all the things you've done wrong in your life.

I found myself hiding out under the coffee table until things calmed down. The cat was also taking shelter there and as we made eye contact, she glared at me as if to say, "Yeah, that pretty much sucks, huh?" I returned to the bedroom in hopes of seeking an apology from the girlfriend but found her fast asleep, likely unaware of the events which had just occurred.

Through Feline Eyes

For as long as I can remember, I've always been a cat owner. I don't remember much about my first cat, Frisco, though I have seen numerous photos of her and me together, so I'm reasonably sure that she actually existed. To this day my parents maintain that one day Frisco went on an adventure and never returned. As a side note, I got the same story from them in regards to a hamster that I once owned. I'm still waiting for my parents to admit that both animals suffered some horrible fate that they kept from me in order to protect my innocence. The next cat we had, "Ornery," belonged to my sister. She kept up with everyone for a good nineteen or twenty people years before succumbing to old age. The cat that I had at around the same time, named "Scamp," had adopted us while my family was out for a walk one evening. She followed us home and just never left. I moved away to college and left her behind, eventually receiving a sad phone call from my mother to let me know that Scamp had had an unfortunate encounter with the tires of my mom's SUV. Due to my father's vocal disapproval of the feline species, all of my pets had lived outside, forbidden to enter the house at any time.

When I met my girlfriend, whom I had also followed home and never left, she was in the process of pet hunting for a house cat. Before I knew it, a beautiful gray Maine coon cat, with the extremely feminine name of "Pom Pom" had entered the equation. After just several months of sharing a small apartment with the animal, I started to understand my father's reasoning to keep the cats outside. Pom Pom is still with us to this day, and frankly, it's not that she makes a bad indoor pet; it's just that somewhere early on she made it her life's goal to passive-aggressively torture us and destroy everything that we care about inside the home.

I've often wondered what it would be like to go through a day in the life of Pom Pom. I imagine that the first order of business would be to wake my girlfriend promptly at four o'clock in the morning by lying on her face. The lack of air in her lungs would cause her to animate, gasping for air. I would let out a squeal to tell her, "Oh, cool, you're awake. How about you get your lazy bones out of bed and fill that empty food bowl that I saw in the kitchen?" I would then run across her body multiple times at high speeds until she complied. Once I had eaten my fill, I would show her my appreciation by intertwining myself between her legs, knocking her to the floor as she headed back toward the bed.

The second order of business would be to holler loudly to show her that I was now thirsty. I would whole-heartedly believe that the stagnant water in the dish next to the food bowl was not up to my standards and remember that she should know by now that I only drink out of the bathroom sink. When she ignored these suggestions, I would give her a second, subtler hint by jumping up onto the bathroom counter and from there I would face the mirror and attempt to bat my reflection into oblivion with my claws. This commotion would cause her to rise once again and turn on the sink. After my thirst was quenched, I would wait for her to lie back down and would thank her for the drink by once again lying on her face.

When she finally arose to prepare for the day at work, I would naturally assume that it was time to play. If she didn't immediately grab the elastic string with the feathers on the end and wave it around my face, I would get her attention by creeping up behind her and sinking my claws deep into the back of her thigh. My small cat brain would lead me to believe that this action tickled. If I wasn't done playing when she took off to do other things, I would either sit in the middle of the floor and go to work loudly cleaning my bottom with my own mouth (a tactic also perfect for clearing out unwanted house guests) or try to occupy myself by making an effort to free climb the drapery in the bedroom. As the curtain rod came crashing down, breaking precious mementos from her youth, I would be alarmed by the situation and attempt to get as far away as possible. In my haste to escape, I wouldn't see the power cord attached to the television set and would run right into it, causing it to be wrapped around my body. By the time my girlfriend arrived on the scene to investigate the noise, I would be in the other room with whatever was left of the TV that I had pulled off the entertainment center and dragged along with me, pretending as though I had nothing to do with the mess in question. This would be, of course, a charade that I had spent countless days perfecting.

Chapter 5:

Sometimes My Imagination Gets the Best of Me

One Day the Robots Will Come for Us All

E ver since the robot was first invented, there have been people who swear up and down that this marks the first step towards the fall of man. They claim that if we ever manage to perfect the art of creating a synthetic humanoid with the right combination of emotion, mobility, and free will, that it's only a matter of time until that humanoid develops self-awareness, realizes its potential as the superior being, and proceeds to enslave the human race. To be fair, their arguments are backed with scientific fact taken from documentary films such as *The Terminator*, *The Matrix*, and *RoboCop*.

I try not to stress about things outside of my control. My suggestion would be to focus on the present and worry about the robots we have in our lives now, rather than the ones who may eventually hunger for the destruction of the world.

More and more I see new devices introduced into our society and households that automate some of life's simpler functions. You may be familiar with the Roomba, a small disc-shaped robot that will vacuum your floors at a designated time and then return itself to its charging station. In the eyes of the robot naysayer, the Roomba would also prove useful in sneaking up onto the owner's face in the middle of the night to vacuum the final breaths from his or her lungs. There's another up- and-coming robot called the Automower, which is a four-wheeled device that will mow your lawn without the need for human steering. Anti-robot activists are quick to point out that pairing a rather unintelligent robot with a lawnmower blade is a guaranteed way to have your body parts chopped off. You may even be familiar with Wakamaru, the Japanese companion robot designed for the elderly, which can, for the most part, understand human speech and will even call 911 in the case of an emergency. Robotophobes will remind us of that one isolated incident during the beta test process where a Wakamaru laughed and mocked its elderly owner as she lay seizuring on the floor.

The aforementioned robots are highly advanced and are pushing the technological envelope but are not readily available to just anyone. Personally, I would worry more about the robots we deal with on a regular basis. There's one in particular that I think we should keep a careful eye on because you never know when it will turn on you. Of course, I'm talking about the cheeky British robot that lives inside my GPS device.

Global positioning systems are becoming a regular staple in vehicles across America, and nine out of ten cellular phones have them built right in. A few weeks ago while driving into unfamiliar territory, I missed a turn that the GPS robot voice was very adamant I take. She had no qualms about letting me know that she was heavily burdened by the task of recalculating my directions and, as I repeatedly missed the intersection, the more serious her robotic tone became. I was starting to worry that before long she would be feeding me directions that would cause me to unintentionally drive into a nearby lake, or worse, I had visions of the British robot turning the GPS unit off completely, but not before spouting a final comment of "Now arriving in the bad part of town."

Coffee: The Gateway Drug

Lately I've found myself experiencing an increased feeling of energy and alertness, an elevated mood, and a feeling of supremacy. This has been paired with irritability, paranoia, restlessness, extreme anxiety, high levels of energy and excited, exuberant speech. My friends tell me that these are symptoms of cocaine use, but as it turns out, they are also the side effects of coffee.

I was never a fan of coffee growing up. Sure, my mother drank it, but I could never understand the appeal and had a hard time getting past the taste. Once I was living on my own, I finally succumbed to peer pressure and drank several cups of black coffee late one night. I was told that all the cool kids were doing it and that if I drank coffee, then I would look older. Being young and naïve, I found it impossible to say no. Surprisingly, it was quite delicious that time around and not so surprisingly, it caused me to stay awake for three days straight.

From there on out it was a long, dark, lonely road and I began selling my personal belongings and taking poorly planned cash advances just to get my Starbuck's fix. It was no longer just an early morning pick-me-up but a full-blown addiction. Soon I was partaking between meals to keep the energy levels high, drinking it at work to stay focused, and even sipping the brew late at night when the rest of the world was sleeping so I could stay up late and catch re-runs of "Quantum Leap." The beans kept getting darker, and before I knew it, I was a complete slave to the grinder and my Brew-

Master 5000. Eventually I was making coffee so thick that it had to be chewed, and I was prone to going on week-long Dunkin Donuts binges. I knew that it was a bad sign when I started importing the heavy duty Colombian stuff and spent my days drinking away my income. It was only a matter of time until I ditched the dark mountain roast and moved on to more exotic stuff like lattes and espresso.

Finally, after months upon months of being locked inside my apartment, alternating between jumping rope while reciting Shakespeare a la the Micro Machines man, and sitting on the couch shaking and sweating profusely while hallucinating about giant cockroaches stealing my Q-Tips, I was ready to admit that I had a problem.

Recently my friends and loved ones hosted an intervention to once and for all separate me from the beans. They sat me down, told me how much they loved me, and explained that I had become a much different person. They confessed that things just hadn't been the same since my attention span reduced itself to a mere half a second, and they were finding it rather disturbing that I could no longer blink. I agreed to attend regular support meetings to help me get through the trying time. However, at the very first Caffeine-Anonymous meeting, which only lasted five minutes, there must have been a mix up with the refreshments order because in the back next to the muffins and behind the lemonade they were serving coffee.

How Many Gum Balls in the Jar? I Don't Care.

Do you remember that game you would play back in grade school where the teacher would ask the class to guess how many gum balls were in a jar and whoever had the closest guess would win all the gum balls? I was horrible at that game.

My guess would be something like eighty-five and the correct answer was always closer to four hundred. For as long as I can remember, I've never been able to look at something and estimate how many of that item are there. Not that I'm missing out on a vital life skill or am overly bitter at never winning the aforementioned game, but I'm amazed at my lack of ability, nonetheless.

Recently as I was enjoying some chocolate-covered coffee beans, I took a look at the nutrition information on the side. Imagine my shock when I saw that the recommended serving size for the coffee beans was forty pieces. By the time I had viewed this information, I had only eaten three of them and found myself completely wired and jittery from the caffeine and had pretty much resigned myself to the fact that I wasn't going to sleep for the next week. If I were to sit and chomp down forty of these things, then the evening was bound to end with my heart exploding in my chest.

I noticed that there were supposedly three and a half servings in the container. I'm no mathematician but I believe that three and a half servings would indicate that there were approximately one hundred forty beans in the bag. While looking at the container, my eyes did not calculate one hundred forty beans. Fifty seemed more accurate. That was my guess. That's what I would have written on the little slip of paper and handed in to my teacher. That's the number that would have lost me the game. This lack of being able to estimate the contents of a bag filled with round objects caused my reality to spin out of control and I threw accusations at my girlfriend that the serving size printed on the bag was clearly a mistake because there was no way that there were one hundred forty beans in the bag!

I suddenly began fearing for anyone else that may have purchased a similar box of chocolate-covered coffee beans and attempted to eat forty of them after being fooled by the false facts listed on the box. Due to my body's reaction to the treats, I began to suspect that the real serving size might have actually been just two coffee beans and I had potentially overdosed. Should I induce vomiting? Should I go to a doctor? My world was a lie, the bag was a lie, and I just stood there, unable to estimate the number of beans and too scared to empty the bag and count them one by one. Before I knew it, I had gone into a full-on caffeine-fueled flurry of confusion and extreme paranoia. My eyes began darting around the room looking for answers. They landed on a jar of jellybeans on the table. My brain started its feeble attempts at calculating. It was right around that time that I blacked out.

When I awoke, I realized that on my trip to the floor, I had knocked over the bag of chocolate-covered coffee beans and was now surrounded by a small brown army of irony. As I picked them up, I counted them one by one. In the end there were exactly one hundred thirty-seven. I had lost the game. Again.

4 Out of 5 Dentists Agree: They Enjoy Hurting You

Let me start this off by saying that I hate going to the dentist. Nay, I loathe going to the dentist and after a recent trip to get my teeth cleaned, polished, and back into presentable shape, I had to take a moment to ponder something: did it ever occur to anyone that maybe dentists are just in it for the pain? Please, stop a moment to consider this. The way I see it, if the main tools for your profession include a drill, syringes, and gas, then you're probably more geared for euthanasia than fixing rotting molars. I mean come on, this is clearly a job designed with the sadist in mind.

In case you haven't visited a dentist lately, times have changed. They no longer let you see the doctor right out. Instead, they send in a dental hygienist to get you warmed up for the horror that is to come. It's like a classic gangster movie where the big guy comes in and roughs you up for a bit before the boss comes strolling in and cuts off your hand. Before anything else, the hygienist always decides to take new x-rays for your file. To do this, she makes you bite down on what feels to be a rusted bottle cap, then quickly doses your face with a hefty amount of radiation. From there she scrapes, pokes and flosses your gums into oblivion for a good twenty-five minutes, you know, just to get that taste of blood in your mouth. That's the taste of inevitability.

Soon after the first round of abuse ends, you skip to the main event where the dentist comes in and gives you a big handshake and a smile. This smile is just a façade to hide the true evil he hides within. He puts the surgical mask on his face and straps the ball gag on yours. Before you know it, you have a needle poking your gums rapidly like a semi-automatic weapon and the sound of the drill fills your eardrums. After spending forty-five minutes in the recliner of doom gazing into the bright white light, while wishing that angels would appear from it and whisk you away from your torture, you might find yourself wondering why dentists wear those surgical masks. I have solved that mystery and let me tell you, it's so that you can't see them smile as you squirm in pain. Why do you think they ask you questions when your mouth is full of gauze, cotton and anesthetic? It's a joke that never gets old to them. Once in a while through the tears, you will see shapes that resemble faces floating over yours and they'll ask you the big question: "Are you doing all right?" Since there are two hands in your mouth, the only way to answer the query is with the single tear that streams from your eye to your chin. They love that part.

Eventually the torture ends and they attempt to teach you a life lesson by saying, "If you would floss better then we wouldn't have to do this."

Not only have they destroyed your face, but also your self-confidence. When all is said and done, you have to pay these people for the pain they have inflicted and then you return home and spend the rest of the day wishing that you could feel your mouth, lips, tongue, nose, and eyeballs as you try to drink liquid from a straw and watch it all dribble back out. Each time this happens, a dentist somewhere smiles behind his surgical mask.

Haiku Poetry

I've never been interested in poetry. I understand how it's a valuable form of self-expression to some writers and wouldn't want to devalue that; however, I've never been able to wrap my head around some forms, most notably, the kind known as Haiku. Haiku is a Japanese model, which consists of three metrical phrases containing five syllables, then seven, and then five again. These short poems are usually scattered and have no discernible plot to them. I find that they leave me, an unfulfilled reader, with questions and without closure. After pondering why Haiku does not appeal to me, I realized that maybe it's not that I don't respect the form itself, but rather I believe that poets who work in this style are just afraid to commit to finishing what they start.

In an attempt to branch out into different forms of writing, I've written a Haiku poem which will also help to illustrate my point:

This is my poem
I'm kind of sleepy right now
I'll finish this soon

Going Green –
To the Extreme

With a new year, a new President, and a new haircut, I feel that it's time that I also adopt a new attitude towards the environment. Like many others I have recently found myself living in complete and utter terror of what's happening to our environment and ecosystems. Frankly, it's scarier than any horror movie ever released. I have crawled out from under the blankets, where I was busy trembling in fear with my flashlight, long enough to share with you six ways that I will be attempting to go Green!

I've done the research and read numerous articles on how to successfully go Green. In fact, I've read so many Green tips that it's possible that I may have gone blind in my left eye, and I'm willing to bet that losing my eyesight somehow helps the environment, so I don't even plan on seeing a doctor. What follows is the list I have compiled that will lead me on my journey towards saving the environment.

Green Tip #1: Conserve Energy

The most common way that various websites encouraged my first steps into Green-dom was by finding opportunities around the house to conserve energy. Suggestions ranged from simple things, like turning off the lights when leaving the room, to more advanced techniques such as installing energy-saving light bulbs in my lamps. Being a middle of the road type of guy, I decided that I too could help do my part in conserving energy by unplugging excess electronics around the home. Computers, TV's, and stereo systems aren't in constant use and don't need to be suckling at the power teat. However, while adapting to this new lifestyle I will develop an annoying habit of only unplugging these devices while they are in use by my girlfriend. She will become frustrated by my actions and in turn I will accuse her of being un-American. After several weeks of having to plug and unplug miscellaneous electronics around my apartment, the extremist that lies dormant within me like a hibernating bear will surface and in one swift and poorly thought out moment will decide that not paying the power bill is the easiest way to go Green. This will ultimately cut down on my power consumption when thirty days later my world plunges into total darkness.

Green Tip #2: Reduce Waste Output

Another stop on the road to Green-land was listed as managing waste output. This makes complete sense, but what waste am I producing that I could cut from my life? Then it hit me. I would make an effort to completely remove toilet paper from my everyday routine. I buy it, use it, and then it's flushed to the big sewer in the sky. I decided that after I had my morning coffee and the time was right, I would spend five to ten minutes hiking around outside seeking out a valid toilet paper replacement. This could come in the form of anything earthly, from leaves, to pine cones, to mulch, or even stray cats. All completely biodegradable items to boot. During this process I will cut down on my waste output and at the same time make any house guests with indigestion extremely uncomfortable.

Green Tip #3: Conserve Water

One pro-Green website wasn't shy when it came to the importance of water conservation. While the most common suggestion was to avoid purchasing bottled water, where the plastic bottle then becomes waste, they suggested instead keeping a water filter pitcher in the refrigerator. I realized that I had already gone Green in this aspect of my life. This was unacceptable since I was on a mission to improve, and staying static was not an option. I was going to have to kick it up a notch and attempt a daring feat that even stunt master Evel Knievel would find daunting… I would have to go Greener. Thankfully, NASA made this a no-brainer for me. Recently the news has been flooded with information regarding the high tech urine converter that was built for the International Space Station. This device was designed to do exactly what its name suggestions: convert human urine into clean drinking water. Sadly, after months of testing, the system still didn't function correctly, but after NASA works out the kinks, it's only a matter of time until it hits the home market. I will begin saving my pennies now and be first in line to purchase my home urine converter the day they hit the shelves. This will end up saving me heaps of money on my water bill each month, but due to a glitch in the converter I will be admitted to the hospital the following year due to drinking my own urine.

Green Tip #4: Recycle

An article called "10 Easy Ways to Go Green" suggested that I create a community compost pile and then involve the other inhabitants of my apartment complex. That's an easy way to a Greener life? I don't even talk to my neighbors, let alone believe that we could bond together under the common cause of creating a biodegradable junk pile. I think whoever wrote the article confused "Apartment Complex" with "Commune." Having never spoken to anyone else in my building, I'm trying to envision just how this conversation with my next-door neighbors would go. Would they be into it? Would they be as excited to help the environment as I am? Or would they kick me in the groin and as I'm doubled over, give me an atomic wedgie like those guys in high school did? I decided that the answer was better left to fate. As I knock on their door I can only speculate that upon their answering I would say to them something like: "So guys, I was thinking, we should totally take all our biodegradable items... and just throw them in a pile out here! What do you say?"

My attempt to follow up that question with a high-five of approval will be met with a door slamming in my face. I will realize that I could have probably phrased the question better. Over the next several weeks I will pile rotten food, used cat litter, and my earnest collection of toilet paper leaves in a pile next to the apartment's mailboxes. I will champion my new found Green lifestyle while everyone else champions my eviction. Eventually, they will win.

Green Tip #5: Reduce Usage of Cleaning Supplies

I was completely caught off guard when I read that using cleaning supplies from the store were taking their toll on the environment. Apparently, by using the same old multi-purpose cleaners we are making the bacteria immune to the cleansers and in fact are only making the bacteria stronger. The article had several suggestions for how to create your own cleaning solvents from stuff you might already have in that dank cupboard under your sink that gives you a headache every time you open it. The most popular do-it-yourself cleaning supplies came from different combinations of baking soda and vinegar. This will end up keeping the super-germs at bay, but while mixing my home disinfectant I will become distracted and instead use the vinegar and baking soda to create a homemade erupting volcano model like the one I entered in the science fair back in seventh grade.

Green Tip #6: Find Alternate Methods of Transportation

The number one way to go Green didn't come as a shock, but it definitely proved itself to be the most difficult to conform to. Apparently by driving my automobile around town I am destroying everything environmental that is within eyesight. Now, if I was really going to commit to going green, then I was going to have to cut back, if not cut out, my fossil fuel consumption. At first, I wasn't completely sure how I was going to do it, but then it became obvious: I was going to beat the system. The way I see it, just because I can't use gas doesn't mean I can't use the car itself. If I could find a gas-free way to propel the vehicle, then I was still following the rules.

Technicalities aside, my game plan was this: I would locate and purchase two blowtorches from a hardware store, then somehow fashion an economy sized can of hairspray, with extra strong hold, to each one. After mounting these contraptions on my back bumper, I would proceed to cleverly rewire my car so when I push the accelerator, it would depress the spray nozzles causing them to shoot their contents into the flames of the blowtorches. In a perfect world, this would create some sort of rocket booster propulsion effect, seen only in the minds of the most naive of children, that would shuttle me forward at high velocities. During my initial stroke of genius, I will forget to design a stronger brake apparatus and as I'm sailing off the highway and into a lake, I will recall that I actually know nothing about auto mechanics. Even later I will realize that aerosols of any kind are in fact destroying the ozone and I will have been defeated at my own game.

Soon after this defeat I will purchase a bicycle in one final attempt to Green-up my transportation. After a few weeks of cruising the sidewalks and jockeying for position amongst the million other bikers in the zip code, I will experience an epiphany as I accidentally crash into a homeless man and sail over my handlebars into a nearby dumpster: the bike is cutting down on my pollution output, but eureka! I can go even Greener! I will then purchase a unicycle from a shady dwarf that I located through a newspaper advertisement found in said dumpster and will proceed to zoom around my former cycling brethren and ridicule them for wasting rubber resources by having front tires and chastise them for polluting the environment. I will then suffer a brutal beating at the hands of annoyed bikers in really tight elastic pants.

The Perfect Valentine's Day Gift

It's that time of year again and Valentine's Day is upon me. Like most men, I procrastinated until the last minute on getting a present for my girlfriend, so after a quick anxiety attack and the collection of pillows for my upcoming nights relegated to the couch, I did what every fellow in this situation does and consulted the Internet to be my guide into finding the perfect gift. After a few quick runs through a search engine, I found myself on a website which promised to list three fantastic gift ideas. A smile appeared on my face after seeing the first suggestion. I knew right then I had found just the thing. And by "just the thing" I mean "possibly the weirdest gift idea ever."

The website's suggestion led me to a website where you are able to order a personalized fantasy novel. Yes, you read correctly and that look on your face is the same one I had on mine. Unless of course you're smiling, and saying to yourself, "Wow, this really is the best thing I've ever heard!" in which case that's the complete opposite of the reaction I had. Everyone knows how much women enjoy a good fantasy novel. The industry makes billions every year. Walk into any bookstore and cruise down the Romance aisle and you will see countless women browsing the back covers of these naughty novels and then throwing them back onto the shelves, turning beet red with embarrassment, and walking in the opposite direction the second that they make eye contact with you.

This particular website offered upwards of twenty-five stock fantasy books that you are able to personalize to your liking by submitting the names of you and your sweetheart, your pet names for one another, favorite locations and many other trivial bits of information. For just fifty bucks they will paste it all into a paperback book and ship it to your door. For an extra fee you can even get your pictures on the cover to really bump up the realism. As any fantasy novel addict will tell you, and this information came from additional Internet research that made me uncomfortable to read, there are the "mild" fantasy novels that women keep on the bookshelf and enjoy a few pages of before going to bed at night, and then there are the "wild" novels that they keep under the bed in a shoe box and only take out when the door is locked and absolutely no one else is around. The level of naughty that you want your custom book to contain is completely customizable. I really had to consider if this was something I wanted to give to my favorite girl as a token of my love and appreciation. I have never seen her read a romance novel; however, I tend to believe generalizations. I let the situation play out in my mind in order to help me make the final decision.

Chances are that since it's so close to Valentine's Day I would have to order the book, and pay the extra cash to have it over-nighted to my apartment, and place it directly from the mailbox into the decorative gift bag I'd bought, and subsequently straight into the hands of my girlfriend. Since she enjoys reading, she would likely skip off immediately to dive into it. I would chuckle to myself, knowing what she was in store for and eagerly anticipate her reactions to the characters within.

During the rest of the day I would not disturb her and risk interrupting the magic that was happening within the pages. Once in a while when she would happen to glance up at me from the couch where she's absorbing the novel, she would display a questioning look as if to say, "How in the world did you pull this off?" I would simply smile back mischievously, eager for her to finish reading so that I could hear the overall reaction. Several hours later I'd hear the front cover of the book bump shut, the typical action she takes when finishing up a novel, and I would prepare to receive a warm embrace in thanks for the sultry literary journey she had just taken. Perhaps the romance from the novel would work its way into a real life setting.

My girlfriend hitting me across the face with the book would be the first indication that something was amiss. As I lay on the floor clutching my face and rolling from side to side she would ask me questions such as, "What kind of sick joke is this?" and "Are you trying to be funny?" She would drop the book onto my chest and storm into the bedroom, slamming the door behind her. Completely confused, I'd pick myself up off the ground, grab the book and relocate to a nearby chair where I'd open the cover to see what the problem was. Much to my dismay, I would spot the title page hidden behind the perverse cover and realize that the book I had given my girlfriend as a sign of my affection wasn't *Island of Love* as intended but instead I had received a misprint from the printer and the book within was actually, *The Shining* by Stephen King.

Thinking that with my luck, this is exactly what would happen, I decided to head back to the initial search results and continue my hunt for the perfect gift.

Wheel of the Fortunate

R ecently my best friend auditioned for the television trivia game show *Jeopardy*. He's a smart fellow who has always dreamed of appearing on a knowledge-based trivia game show. This of course caused me to ponder which game show I would audition for if given the opportunity. It would have to be a game that did not require strong knowledge on various worldly subjects, took little or no athletic skill, and was based mostly on pure luck. Right then, I knew the perfect game show I would audition for: *Wheel of Fortune*.

I surfed on over to the official *Wheel of Fortune* website where I was greeted by a large picture of hosts Pat Sajak and Vanna White standing in front of the giant Wheel. Their eyes seemed to burn holes directly into my soul as I searched for the audition link. Once it was located I entered my personal information and was asked to fill out answers to a series of questions. This should be easy enough considering I made it past the eighth grade. Right off the top I could choose to express my interest in participating for one of their theme week events that they sprinkled throughout the year to add additional excitement to a game based around spinning a large wheel. These options consisted of Family Week, Best Friends Week, Sweethearts Week, or Armed Forces Week. I thought for a second before choosing the button that could ultimately change my financial destiny. I'm not in the armed forces, so that's out, and if I took my family on the show then they would likely spend more time embarrassing me than shouting out letters of the alphabet. Best Friends week could be an option if I could guarantee that my buddy wouldn't be too busy playing *Jeopardy* and schmoozing with Alex Trebek, so I chose Sweetheart's Week and decided that if I were chosen for the event, then I would spring this news on my girlfriend while she was sleeping and convince her later that she had agreed to it.

Over the course of the next thirty questions I had to inform them of which professional sports I was interested in, which of course, allowed me to bypass seventy percent of the application. I was also unable to answer the questions regarding my favorite country music star or favorite soap opera actors and failed to see how these answers were connected to my being able to guess words for money. I was, however, able to answer yes when asked if I had any pets. With my two answers filled in and feeling the total opposite of confident, I submitted the form to the powers that be.

On the next page I was informed that over one million people have entered to be on *Wheel of Fortune* and fewer than six hundred have been chosen, so I probably shouldn't hold my breath. They also discouraged waiting by the phone or showing up at Pat Sajak's home in Los Angeles, pretending to be his long lost Uncle Louie in a sad attempt to be picked as a contestant. It did, however, suggest that just in case I am chosen, prerequisites included that I should be familiar with the English alphabet and be able to call out letters in a loud, confident voice. Pat Sajak recommended that I be decisive when it comes time to spin or solve the puzzle, and Vanna added that I should strike a good balance between calling out consonants and buying vowels, as it makes for an exciting game.

For several weeks I ignored Sajak's advice and waited by the phone. When it never rang I was forced into the realization that I'm just not good enough to call out letters in a television studio. I turned on the television to preoccupy my mind and was greeted with a new episode of *The Price Is*

Right. I immediately ran to the computer to find their audition form.

Escalator Etiquette

As an American I am exposed to things every day that make me extremely uncomfortable: the constant threat of terrorism, global warming, fast food, FOX news, and of course Tyra Banks. I recently discovered something else that makes my stomach churn more than accidentally landing on Bill O'Reilly's television show while channel surfing: people running up behind me on escalators.

Escalators make me uneasy in the first place. It might be because I don't enjoy jumping onto things while they are in motion, or maybe I just don't trust machines. More so it's probably because while I was growing up, I remember countless public service announcements played throughout my Saturday morning cartoons that warned me of the dangers associated with these machines. There was one in particular that sticks out in my memory where it was demonstrated how the gaps on the sides of the escalator stairs could easily suck in a rubber pencil eraser, and how your shoelaces could also get caught in the same area, causing them to get stuck in the motor, which in turn would drag you under the stairs to suffer the most gruesome and embarrassing of deaths. Even though we all know that most PSA's are just out to scare us straight, this one clearly left some emotional scarring.

There are two classes of escalator users. First, there's rider personality A, who is perfectly sane and strolls onto the landing to enjoy a nice, relaxing and stress free, motorized ride to the top. I'm ninety-nine percent sure that this is how the inventor of the escalator intended for the device to be used in the first place. This is completely acceptable and follows all rules and protocols. Rider personality B is someone who gets on the escalator and immediately runs as far up as many of the stairs as he can until he either reaches the top or ends up stuck behind someone. Rider personality B people clearly confuse an escalator with a regular flight of stairs. This is unacceptable.

When riding the escalator with a type B personality, I am beyond uncomfortable when I am midway up my ride and the eager beaver behind me starts to sprint upward in an attempt to set some kind of escalator land speed record. Before I know it, he is on the step directly behind me, breathing down my neck, huffing and puffing to make it very apparent that he is frustrated by the fact that I am standing still. How dare I not walk up the stairs that are already moving of their own accord? Trust me, we're all going to get to the top eventually. Apparently, by invading my personal space bubble, type B's are under the assumption that they can bully me out of the way. It's a shame they are not familiar with my world-class stubbornness.

As the ride progresses, Mr. Escalator Rider Personality Type B will continue to drop subtle hints that I will continue to subtly ignore. First, the fake yawn comes into play to demonstrate how bored he is with not being able to continue up the stairs that are already moving. The second hint, which I've seen happen in the past, is a casual glance at his wristwatch, which is really anything but casual. It's a very over-dramatic move where the arm must stretch far out and elongate completely before being brought back around to where the watch can be placed mere inches from his nose where he will then stare at it intently. The third and final hint comes in the form of an attempt to pass the person or persons in front of him. Wait. Hold the phone. I'm relatively certain that escalator etiquette dictates that under no circumstance should you pass someone while the stairs are in motion, and I am pretty sure that breaking this rule is punishable by death. Need I remind everyone again that we are already moving?

The next time that I encounter Rider Personality B, I will let him play his game. I will let him drop his hints and huff and puff, and when his last-ditch effort comes into play and he attempts to pass me, I will turn around and push him. I'm not out to injure or harm, but I will give him a shove with just enough velocity, which will be predetermined by a well-calculated mathematical equation (solved by someone else, since I am awful at mathematics), so that he topples slowly backwards down the never-ending flight of stairs forever.

Park Ninjas

S everal weeks ago while on a lunch break from work, I
drove by a park and noticed a group of people lined up,
waving their arms and legs in unison. For the life of me, I
couldn't figure out what they were doing. In fact, I had never
seen anything quite like it before. I slowed down a bit and from
what I could gather, they were going through some sort of
martial arts motions. I watched them for a few moments and
then continued on, perplexed by what I had just seen.

Upon my return to work I told an employee about what
I had experienced. He passed it off like it was nothing special
and explained that they were most likely doing Tai Chi, which
is an internal Chinese martial art that some people practice for
health reasons. This explanation made sense; however I felt
just a little bit embarrassed since I had spent the drive back
from lunch excitedly calling all of my friends to tell them that
there were people in the park fighting invisible ninjas.

If Children Were More Like Ewoks, I Might Actually Want Some

I'm not a fan of kids. I use the term "kids" very loosely. In reality, I'm not a fan of anyone under the age of eighteen, and even then, it's sketchy.

I've gotten to the age where I now have friends who've produced babies of their own and apparently they are under the impression that my dislike of under-developed life forms is a disease or a sickness that can be cured by shoving their baby in my face. Let me tell you, this is not a prescription that will help the cause. Even my mother has never understood my negative attitude towards one day having children of my own. She always argues, "You don't like children? What if I had felt the same way?" to which my canned response was always, "Then I guess I'd be someone else's kid."

Recently though, I admitted to myself that maybe having children wouldn't be so bad... if they were more like Ewoks. You might remember the Ewoks from the 1983 classic film *Star Wars: Return of the Jedi*. They were the short furry creatures that helped Han Solo take down the Empire on the forest moon of Endor. It's basic logic: if kids were more like Ewoks, they would prove more useful in life and would be able to perform simple tasks like fending off any attackers to my home by using homemade spears, or creating herbal medicines when the adults fall ill. After all, they are resourceful little creatures. As children they would also be furry, which would increase the likelihood of my wanting to spend time with them or have physical contact on any level. Also, you may or may not know this, but Ewoks are not capable of coherently reproducing the English language. This would prove handy later in life when they wanted to borrow the car or needed cash from their old man.

Occasionally, families enjoy getting together to take cute family photos that will later be put onto the faces of their Christmas cards. Tell me that getting a card with a picture of my wife and me surrounded by numerous Ewoks wouldn't be the best gift ever. Other holidays would be just as fun. Each year come October, this would be the perfect excuse for me to dress up as Han Solo to go out Trick or Treating with the kids at Halloween. Eventually they would want to put on real costumes, so please consider how hilarious it would be to see an Ewok dressed up as a Power Ranger.

Now, I'm sure this makes me sound like I'm a horrible person just out to exploit my Ewok children, and maybe that's true, but how often in your life would you be able to say to your kids, "Just remember guys, you have to be home by six o'clock tonight so we can ceremoniously burn Darth Vader's remains"?

Please, keep your babies out of my face.

J-E-A-L-O-U-S-Y...
Jealousy.

I'm a little jealous of all of the opportunities that children get in life. They have events in their day-to-day lives that we adults rarely get the chance to participate in as we get older.

While in school, the kids get recess, a time for burning off excess energy by running around and acting like fools. This makes adults jealous because we get out of work at six o'clock in the evening and only get to burn off our paychecks by paying bills. Children have the opportunity to learn from their teachers and absorb a wealth of knowledge. Adults? We're jealous because we make crucial mistakes and hope to learn from them but rarely do. Kids have lunch served to them with a balanced diet in mind to keep them healthy. Adults are jealous because most of us can't cook so instead we swing by a drive-thru window for lunch and hope for the best, except for those adults who are in prison, in which case they get the balanced meals served to them daily in order to keep them alive to carry out their sentences. Most adults aren't very jealous of that last part. Above all, the number one opportunity adolescents get that we adults are jealous of is the opportunity to participate in spelling bees.

Okay, so maybe all adults aren't jealous of the spelling bee opportunity, but I sure am. During our middle school years we were forced into such competitions alongside our classmates in an attempt to show off our knowledge, or if we were poor with words, to be humiliated in front of an auditorium full of our friends. Once we're grown, where does a person go to have this chance again?

I did some research and found out that there are a whopping two adult spelling bees offered in the entire United States. One is located in California and the other is found in Texas. These community events apparently happen no more than once a year. That's not often enough for me. I'm jealous that these events are readily available to citizens of those respective states, but I need something that is always ready and waiting whenever I'm looking to get my spelling fix. What I need is to find a seedy place that hosts illegal underground spelling bees. This concept would be similar to the underground poker spots. You buy into the spelling bee for a hefty price, and then take a seat and wait for things to start rolling. Eventually, the winner of the bee would take home the pot and have unparalleled bragging rights for the remainder of the week, not to mention some extra walking around money.

The downside to this concept is that you occasionally hear on the news about underground poker games getting stormed by the police. I could just envision how different it would be to raid an illegal spelling bee versus a poker game. As the authorities kicked down the door, they wouldn't find cards, poker chips, alcohol, or women doing nefarious things in a rundown basement; instead they'd just find a couple rows of folding chairs filled with nerdy-looking adults who are sitting quietly waiting for their turn to spell difficult words. More than likely I would be up at the microphone when the sting happened, making an attempt at spelling "immunoelectrophoretically" for the championship win.

Ultimately I would end up losing the spelling bee because their sudden and alarming entrance would cause me to misspell the word as "I-M-M-U-N-O CRAP!" and as the rest of the contestants ran for the doors, windows, and various secret escape tunnels we had dug prior to starting the competition, the only one left to pay for the crime would be me.

Officers in riot gear would tackle me to the musty floor and the detective working the case would kneel down beside me and ask what the big pile of money in the box was for. I would look at him, puzzled and ask, "Money? Can you please use it in a sentence?"

He would not think this was funny.

I'd be jealous that I didn't get the opportunity to finish spelling my word, but on the bright side, I would be getting those daily balanced meals after all.

Chapter 6:

*Apartment Living,
or 500 Square Feet of
White Walls and Sterility*

Slayer of Roaches,
Savior of Women

I awoke at eight o'clock one morning to find myself on the receiving end of a full on cockroach onslaught. This beast was obviously armed with an unquenchable thirst for my blood, and it was quickly becoming apparent that no amount of flailing and girlish shrieking was going to stop it.

It was an interesting sensation, having those six legs scurry over my bare chest, and, on a much deeper level, made me appreciate waking up instead to the racket of my alarm clock. Since I wasn't wearing my glasses, therefore making me legally blind in three states, I had to first identify the blurry threat before I could create a strategy on how to deal with my pre-coffee assailant. Was it a mouse? Nope, too small. Was it a spider? Nah, not enough legs. Was it my uncle? I doubt it; I haven't seen him in years. I could make out just enough legs and antennae to correctly identify it as the "Periplaneta Americana," which loosely translated into English means "Cockroach of Doom."

After calming myself down with visions of miniature Snickers bars and former high school classmates on fire, I collected my thoughts and proceeded to strip seventy percent of the sheets and blankets from the bed in an attempt to locate the critter and then watched angrily as it bolted and took cover underneath a nearby piece of furniture. After about ten minutes of trying to coax it out from the depths of the dresser-turned-makeshift-insect-fallout-shelter, I had almost given up hope.

Then that's when the creature made a fatal mistake by rearing its ugly head for a split second in an attempt to taunt me. I acted instinctively, forgoing the can of Raid I had on hand, and instead haphazardly slammed that sucker into oblivion with my shoe.

Normally, I don't get an ego about things, but I threw my hands in the air in a manner that would have made Rocky Balboa feel lazy. Cleanup tissue in one hand, roach-coated sandal in the other, I knew at that moment what it must feel like to be the Pope. For that split second I was bigger than The Beatles. For that moment in time... I was the Walrus. I was the one. The Roachslayer. All insects within a two-mile radius quivered with fear and lost control of their bowels.

Where There's Smoke There's... Mulch Fires?

As happens every so often around any type of apartment complex, hired landscaping crews will come along to trim the trees, plant new flowers, blow the leaves, spend most of their day on break smoking cigarettes, and eventually they will lay down new mulch. Last Monday was one of those every so often type days.

I came home from work and saw that all of the sickly looking brown mulch had been replaced with a noticeably brighter kind that contrasted nicely to the drab gray color of my apartment building. The smell of the fresh mulch lingered in the air and coated my nostrils with an aroma that smelled faintly of burnt hair and old Chinese food.

The following day my girlfriend took a stroll out to the mailbox and came back with a wild look in her eyes and told me that in her travels she had come across a pile of mulch that was on fire. Being the good person that she is, she alerted the property manager immediately. Regardless of the fact that the property manager didn't seem to know what to do about it (my first suggestions would have been water or a fire extinguisher), my girl had done her civic duty. Over the course of the next few days there was an epidemic of mulch fires happening all over the complex. Nothing too serious, but in passing you could occasionally spot plumes of smoke rising from the ground around the trees and bushes. Was the hot sun setting our mulch on fire? Had small volcanoes, which had lain dormant for thousands of years, suddenly opened up? Did we have a mulch arsonist on the loose? These were questions that I could not come up with answers to. At least, none that people would take seriously.

When next it was my turn to get the mail, I saw a sign posted on the community bulletin board, where residents usually advertise things for sale, dull apartment events, upcoming yard sales, and personal ads looking for mates in a quarter-mile radius.

The sign read:

ATTENTION!
(¡ATENCIÓN!)

For the safety of all residents, please do not throw cigarette butts in the mulch. We have had several fires this week. If you see a fire, please call the property manager immediately.

Suddenly I had my explanation for everything. Though it was anticlimactic, it was good to know that we weren't sitting on a scaled-down version of Mount St. Helen's. As I prepared to head back toward my apartment, it hit me that these fires were actually leaving the door open for something that could really bring the residential community together. I produced a pen from my pocket and went to work on the fire warning sign.

While walking away I passed another resident heading over to pick up their mail. I knew that they would also see the sign, but perhaps they would look at these fires in a different light.

After some creative editing the sign now read:

ATTENTION!
(¡ATENCIÓN!)

For the safety of all residents, please do not throw cigarette butts in the mulch. We have had several fires this week. If you see a fire, please call the property manager immediately so that we can organize a killer weenie roast. I'm thinking that if we play our cards right we could also get a drum circle going and Lord knows I haven't participated in a raging drum circle since my college days. I would ask that we leave the hallucinogens at home though. Last time we brought hallucinogens to a drum circle, Alice ended up in a coma and that was a big buzz kill for everyone. Plus, Larry was on some bad 'shrooms and was never the same after the hospital trip.

PS – Bring stuff so that we can make Smores.
Man, they are soooo good, am I right?

My Complex at the
Apartment Complex

A few years ago while living in a second floor apartment, I found myself in one of the most awkward predicaments of my life. On a Saturday afternoon I headed out the door to run some errands. The second I stepped outside onto the balcony, I sensed that something was different. The building hadn't been painted, the neighbors hadn't moved out, and my balcony furniture was still there. Not being able to identify the change, I shrugged off the paranoia and decided to move on with my day. As I went to venture down the stairs, I noticed exactly what had been adjusted. The wooden staircase leading up to my apartment had completely disappeared.

Now, as crazy as it may sound, I found this to be a slight inconvenience. I did what anyone in the same situation would do. I went back inside my apartment, closed the door, waited ten seconds and then reopened it, hoping that I would find my stairs magically restored. As I re-emerged filled with optimism, I was only disappointed. Where the staircase had once been, a big empty gap stared back at me, laughing hysterically. Personally, I didn't think the situation was all that funny.

The only logical explanation was that I was the victim of some epic practical joke by my apartment complex. This didn't make a whole lot of sense since I'd never seen anyone in the office display any signs of a sense of humor during past visits. This led me to consider whether or not I had been late on my rent. Perhaps this was a new passive-aggressive tactic used for money collection. While pacing the porch without a logical answer, I became enraged at the property manager for not giving me some sort of prior notification that this would be happening so that I could plan my life accordingly. I was beyond frustrated. I was seeing red. I was absolutely livid. My mind began to race, and I formulated a plan for breaking my lease and fleeing to a rival apartment complex. I would slander their name across town and not return my laundromat or mailbox keys on my way out.

Forcing myself to cool down and think logically, I began to weigh my options in order to decide how badly I needed to run my errands. I quickly thought up three approaches to getting down to the first floor. My first instinct was to call the fire department, but that only gave me visions of firefighters rescuing cats from trees. I refused to be the proverbial cat. I considered the possibility of jumping from the ledge and grabbing for the large tree several feet away, thinking that I could then climb to the ground. Maybe it would be easier for me to tie the sheets of my bed together and repel down the side of the building. I knew that this wouldn't work since I'm a male and therefore only own one set of sheets. The ideas were good, but seeing as how they required some sort of physical prowess to execute, this only angered me more as I am completely lacking in that department.

I decided that a relaxing day in the apartment was going to be the best course of action. As I turned to go back inside, I noticed something sticking out from underneath my doormat. Upon closer investigation I found it to be a piece of paper, which I pulled out and unfolded. Printed upon the sheet was a memo addressed to me from the apartment complex. It was to inform me that on this particular date, my apartment stairs would be deconstructed due to rotting wood and for my safety they would be replaced within a six-hour period.

Based on the date printed on the corner of the stationery, the note had been hiding out beneath the doormat for roughly two weeks. I decided right then that when I eventually moved elsewhere I was obligated to return the mailbox key to make up for all the bad things I had thought about the complex. I did, however, keep the laundromat key.

Imprisoned in Pajamas

We all have traumatic moments in life that we would like to forget. While most have to do with a rough upbringing and others have to do with failed relationships, mine occurred last August when I got stuck on a first-floor apartment porch.

Now, please don't make assumptions and please don't judge. Getting stuck on one's porch takes talent, finesse, and precise timing. It all started when I stepped outside my apartment with a cold glass of water to enjoy a beautiful Florida day. I grabbed the doorknob to go back in and was faced with a harsh reality: doorknobs are not supposed to turn three hundred sixty degrees. The doorknob was definitely broken, and I was definitely stuck outside.

As I sipped my water, I became aware of my vicious bed-head and current attire, pajamas, which ruled out seeking help from the normal channels, like people. They were likely to think that I was homeless and looking for money. Since I live on the first floor of my apartment building I knew that climbing over the porch wall and walking around to the front door was the best option. However, I had made the mistake of thinking that going outside barefoot was a fantastic idea and the flowerbeds surrounding my porch were full of fresh mulch, which now resembled a field full of razor blades. As I gently lowered myself down onto the miniature spears, tears came to my eyes but I persisted and made it to the front door. As fortune would have it, I had made yet another oversight and realized that even though I had made it to the door, and freedom was just on the other side, my house keys were inside. Logic forced me to remember that even if I did have the keys, my chain lock was still going to hold me at bay.

Defeated, I traversed the field of razors yet again and climbed back onto my porch. Even though there were no keys to be found in my pajama pocket, there was a cell phone. I was able to locate the number for my apartment complex in the contacts list and gave them a dial. To my horror, they had recently closed for the day and thus I was transferred to the emergency service line where a young lady answered who barely spoke any English but was ready to help me out with my emergency needs, as long as I could explain them in short, simple sentences. I had to explain to her that I was stuck on my porch. She had trouble understanding the concept and informed me that there was a fifty-dollar fee for getting locked out after business hours. I had to clarify that I hadn't technically been locked out and it was the door's fault over my own. I worked the victim angle and told her that I was stuck on the porch in my pajamas with no shoes, no keys, and only half a glass of water. She failed to see the seriousness of the situation and informed me that someone would be along in roughly forty-five minutes to let me in. I thought I could deal with that.

The temperature was slowly rising in the late afternoon sun and the water began to taunt me. I knew that even though I would soon be free, I had to ration. This was now a game of survival. Everything I had learned as a member of the Boy Scouts was about to pay off. Then it dawned on me that I had dropped out of Boy Scouts early on, and the only thing I had potentially learned was their code of honor. Even that was foggy with the heat eating away at my brain.

Forty-five minutes went by with no rescue. I once again dialed the emergency service line. The same gal answered and continued to show no sympathy towards my situation. She assured me that help was on the way. I assured her that I was hungry and toying with the notion of eating my hand if no one arrived soon.

Finally, four hours later when I had nearly lost all hope of salvation, the maintenance guy appeared to let me inside. He unlocked the door and had to pulverize the chain lock with a screwdriver. As I hobbled towards the door, my feet nearly bleeding from another trip through the razors, he put out a hand to stop me. He said, "I'm sorry, Sir, our policy states that I can't let you inside the apartment until I see your I.D."

After some quick thinking I explained how I probably had left it in my other pajama pants.

An Alarming Situation

Several weeks ago I was awakened by the worst noise imaginable. It wasn't the vacuum cleaner, it wasn't a police siren, and it wasn't even the voice of Tyra Banks. It was the fire alarm in my apartment building.

Now this wasn't some small-time smoke alarm, this was the building-wide siren that gets triggered when someone drops an atomic bomb on the apartment complex or when Ryan Seacrest becomes the host of yet another television show. This was serious. It all started at four-thirty on Sunday morning. I had just drifted off after a long evening and then suddenly and without warning my brain was being pierced with a sonic assault that caused me more pain than any migraine I've ever experienced. I sat straight up in bed as quick as a bullet while simultaneously one of my cats turned itself inside out and ran straight into a wall, and the other rocketed upward and latched onto the popcorn ceiling.

I'm a rather cynical person, so through the noise I found myself questioning the authenticity of the emergency. In school when we had fire drills, we were always taught to escape a potentially burning building in a quick and orderly fashion; however, since I had been asleep just thirty seconds prior, I took more of a sluggish and confused approach to the evacuation. I swung my feet out of bed and sat for a moment while I rubbed my eyes. I wondered what might be on fire, I wondered if anyone was hurt, and most importantly I wondered if this was important enough for me to have to put on pants.

After wrestling with getting my trousers into place and locating a pair of sandals, I groggily stumbled out the door at the exact same time as the neighbor couple across the way. We exchanged puzzled looks and began to roam around the area to see if we could discover what all the fuss was about. Everything seemed in good shape. The tenants of the entire building were out of their homes in various states of disarray, yet nobody could identify what the emergency was. No one seemed to be injured, nothing had been damaged, and no one was visibly on fire. After several minutes of walking around and being extremely annoyed by it all, my female neighbor decided to call the emergency hotline for the apartment and see if they had the answers we were seeking. After speaking with someone for several minutes and hanging up, she informed the rest of us that she had to go through a call center in India. We knew right then that it was going to be a long night.

We sat in the parking lot for forty-five minutes listening to the siren wail as we all thought about pleasant things or wished for death. Eventually, a fire truck arrived on the scene. The firemen strolled around the building and determined that nothing was on fire. Then they informed the crowd that they could not turn off the alarm as only the apartment maintenance crew had access to where it was housed. They promptly drove off, leaving us once again to contend with the racket on our own. By this time we had amassed a small group of people and spent several minutes getting to know each other, checking each other's ears to make sure they weren't bleeding from the noise, and speculating on the cause of the alarm. Some folks thought that maybe it was a prank while others suggested that perhaps there had been a fire but it had been put out. I suspected that the alarm was triggered to create a poorly timed mixer for the apartment residents.

Eventually, the maintenance crew arrived and was faced with an angry mob dressed in pajamas. Had a lynch mob actually formed, we would have been the most comfortable lynch mob ever. The apartment employees managed to get the alarm turned off and my feeling of anxiety that had persisted for the entire hour finally went away. Our bonding experience was over and the group dispersed. As I was walking through the door into my apartment, the neighbors said something warm and truly heartfelt to me regarding the bonding experience that we had shared... I just couldn't decipher it since I had gone deaf from the alarm.

Mayonnaise!

I might be a criminal, though I am not completely sure. I
haven't committed any type of heinous acts, and no one has
been hurt by my actions; I'm simply just one of those people
who harbors a cat inside his apartment and has yet, after a year
and a half of living there, to inform the property manager. It's
not that I'm trying to live in a dishonest manner, but according
to my lease, if I become an admitted pet owner, then I have to
pay not only a several hundred dollar deposit to the apartment
complex, but I'm pretty sure that they also reserve the right to
harvest some of my bodily organs and get dibs on my first
born. So rather than pony up the cash, I do my best to hide the
animal.

One of the joys of living in an apartment is the
fictitious reasons they feed you in order to invade your living
space. They claim to be checking on various mechanical
functions or to make sure your fire extinguisher still works, but
I see completely through this and have caught onto their game.
What they're really doing is checking to see if you are hiding
animals of any kind. The sketchy thing about these raids on my
home comes from the fact that I get little to no warning when
they are happening. Sometimes it's twenty-four hours,
sometimes it's mere minutes and this leaves me hardly any
time to prepare.

I recently had one of these raids. On the prior night,
upon returning home from work, I found a note on my door
indicating that the following morning a maintenance worker

would be entering my apartment to install a sign on my washing machine that would warn me not to fuss with any of the electrical components or water hoses, something I have yet to this day not thought of doing even in the most boring of times. Regardless of how the words appeared on the page, I was able to decipher the underlying message of "We're going to find that dang cat!"

The following day I was awakened not by the normal racket of my alarm clock, but by a banging on the door, followed by an unintelligible holler. I shot up in my bed and remembered the note I had found the night before. This was it. They were coming in and I had to hide the cat. Before I could move, the knocking on the door became louder and another holler followed. I later realized that the person at the door had been saying "Maintenance," but in my groggy state, coupled with the door that stood between the source and me, it sounded as if they were yelling the word "Mayonnaise." This only added to my overall state of confusion. I had anticipated hiding all cat-related evidence before leaving for work that morning, but time was not on my side. I quickly leapt into action and began picking up miscellaneous cat paraphernalia and tossing it into my bedroom, all the while wondering why I had purchased so many toys and knick-knacks for this animal.

Another knock. "Mayonnaise!"

I knew that eventually the maintenance worker would come inside whether I was home or not, so I had to come up with a stall tactic. I headed for the door and opened it just a crack. Face to face with the maintenance worker, I used my patented excuse for temporarily keeping anyone out of my home. I said, "Please hold on a moment, I just woke up and need to put on some pants." It worked as well as any Jedi mind trick from Star Wars. He smiled and nodded, letting me know that he would come back after inspecting the neighbor's apartment for animals… I mean, installing their warning sign.

I quickly closed the front door and scrambled for the kitchen, collecting the cat's water dish, litter box, and scratch pad, quickly hiding them away. Next came the tricky part, I had to hide the actual cat. Throughout my scurrying, the cat had been wide-eyed on the sidelines, not really comprehending the gravity of the situation. I made eye contact with her and apparently she sensed some sort of danger because she took off running in the opposite direction. I gave chase and my attempts to scoop her up were met with clawing, scratching, hissing, spitting, and a flurry of fur that she is apparently able to loosen from her body on command.

Another knock. "Mayonnaise!"

As I cornered the beast against the oven, I shouted back at the door, "Just a minute!" and dove at the cat. While she gnawed at the tendons of my arm, I transported her to the bathroom, tossing her into my empty bathtub, while wrenching the door closed behind me.

Another knock. "Mayonnaise!"

I was out of time. If I made him wait any longer then he was likely to suspect that I was trying to hide something. I opened the door all the way and invited the man inside to "install a warning sign," and feeling pretty good about having successfully hid any evidence that would finger me as a cat owner. He apologized for catching me at a bad time and than began the walk to my laundry room, his eyes darting all around searching for traces of animal. The installation took only seconds and he was on his way out just moments later. I closed the door behind him, leaning against it to breathe a heavy sigh of relief. When I opened my eyes, I realized that I had left the cat's food bowl out in plain sight. Not only was it in plain sight, but also it was right in the path he had walked to get to my washing machine. I could only hope that he was a cataract sufferer and hadn't noticed. On my way to the bathroom to release my cat from her temporary prison, I saw that my arm was full of puncture wounds from razor sharp feline teeth, and a small stream of blood was leaking its way towards my hand. I calculated the odds of his having seen the blood smear. After opening the bathroom door, I glanced in the mirror only to notice that a giant tuft of cat fur was stuck to my forehead. Maybe the maintenance guy would just assume that I had some sort of rare medical condition that caused me to grow fur, spontaneously bleed, and eat cat food.

Feeling completely defeated and readying my checkbook for the pet security deposit that was likely headed my way, I realized that the maintenance worker had accidentally left his master key ring on my counter. Before I could head outside to catch up with him, a knock at the door froze me in my tracks. "Mayonnaise!"

About the Author

    This book is the brainchild of Weston Locher. It's ironic that he would refer to it as a brainchild because he holds a strong dislike for children. He's an Ohio native who escaped the state because he was tired of being cold and wet in the winter and overheated in the summer. Mostly, he left because his parents refused to believe in the concept of air conditioning. Being the sum of a journalist father and an English teacher mother, he was doomed to a life of writing before he was able to consciously make the decision for himself. He chose to write humor because his family made the mistake of telling him that he was funny. This is further proof of why you shouldn't lie to your children.

    Weston currently resides in Winter Park, Florida.

Made in the USA
Lexington, KY
27 January 2010